THE STRENGTH CONNECTION

How to Build Strength and
Improve the Quality of Your Life

Institute for Aerobics Research
Dallas, Texas

Institute for Aerobics Research
12330 Preston Road
Dallas, Texas 75230

Library of Congress Catalog Card Number
90-83129

ISBN 0-9622206-0-4

Printed in the United States of America

Notice

The information and ideas in this book are for educational purposes and must not be taken as prescriptive advice. Self-treatment can be dangerous, so consult your physician if you have a serious health problem.

The staff of the Institute for Aerobics Research
dedicates this book
with sincere affection
to

Dr. and Mrs. Richard L. Bohannon

Who inspire us daily to achieve excellence
in our personal and professional lives.

CONTENTS

FOREWORD

Over the past 20 years, many people have followed my guidelines for aerobic exercise. I meet people every day who say they read my book, *Aerobics*, in 1968 and it changed their lives. They're still jogging and because of that enjoying all the benefits of an active lifestyle. Some of these people are 60, 70, even 80 years old!

Unfortunately, some of these same people may have neglected other components of fitness. Their bodies look and perform like elite athletes from the waist down but from the waist up they lack the strength to carry their luggage down the airport concourse.

At the Institute for Aerobics Research, we're learning more every day about the importance of strong muscles and bones. The purpose of this book is to emphasize the benefits of balanced fitness: *regular physical activity that includes strength training and flexibility (stretching) in addition to aerobic conditioning.* We think there's a definite connection between adequate muscle strength and endurance, and quality of life.

This book begins with information about the health benefits of balanced fitness. We refer frequently to current research and examine and dispel many of the common myths about exercise, particularly strength training.

In Part II, "How Your Muscles Work," we provide the scientific foundation for planning a strength training program that is both safe and effective. Each time a new scientific term is introduced, it appears in italics. Check the glossary at the end of the book for clear and concise definitions of these terms.

We also felt it was important to include medical information about strength training as an appropriate exercise activity for special groups. In Part III, we discuss the importance of strength training for children and adolescents, women during and after pregnancy, people over 50 and those with chronic diseases such as hypertension, diabetes, heart disease, arthritis and osteoporosis.

We also provide specific strength training recommendations for these groups. Of course, anyone who has special health concerns should talk with his or her physician before beginning an exercise program.

Our research indicates that lack of motivation is the major reason why people don't get as much exercise as they need. Knowing this, we outlined a three step process that will help you to be successful in not simply starting but maintaining a balanced fitness program for life. This process is based on sound principles of behavior modification that begin with self evaluation. These evaluations are appropriate for adults, children and adolescents, so the whole family can participate. We have also included detailed instructions and illustrations for performing the evaluations and easy to read charts for interpreting results.

One of the most fun things about exercise, especially strength training, is the many options available. You can exercise at a health club, a neighborhood fitness facility or at home. You can do calisthenics, work out with hand-held weights or use resistance machines. Your body doesn't know or care how the resistance is applied. The dozens of illustrated exercises included in this book are intended to help you build muscle strength and endurance safely and effectively. We have also included our Strength Points System which is designed to help you quantify your training program.

Congratulations on having accomplished the first step toward a balanced fitness program--investing in this book. Follow these guidelines and recommendations and I know you'll realize the connection between balanced fitness and quality of life, now and in the future.

Good luck to you as you begin your balanced fitness program.

KENNETH H. COOPER, M.D., M.P.H.
Chairman and Founder
Institute for Aerobics Research
Dallas, Texas
July 1990

PART I

THE STRENGTH CONNECTION

BALANCED FITNESS: FROM RESEARCH TO PRACTICE

The role of aerobic exercise in achieving a high level of cardiovascular fitness is well established. Much of the work of the Institute for Aerobics Research over the past twenty years has documented these positive effects. But, there is a need for understanding the benefits of *balanced fitness*. Not just aerobic exercise, although it's extremely important.

A balanced fitness program includes flexibility (stretching) exercises and strength training in addition to aerobic exercise. Balanced fitness is essential to functional fitness and quality of life in the later years, certainly the ultimate goal of every individual.

Meet three people who value their health and fitness:

* Joe is thirty-eight years old and works as a computer software salesman. He played football in college, and except for an old knee injury that bothers him from time to time, he thinks he's in good health. His exercise program consists of heavy weight lifting five days a week.

* Sue, a forty-seven year old mother of three, teaches physical education at an elementary school. She hasn't missed work due to illness during the last year. Running is her favorite exercise. In fact, her training program consists of running 35 to 40 miles per week. She plans to run her first marathon this year.

* Jerry is fifty-six years old and a lawyer by profession. He had
  bypass surgery when he was fifty-two and it changed his life.
  Now he walks briskly for 30-45 minutes three to five days a
  week and spends 30 minutes, three days per week working
  out with light dumbbells at home. To relieve stress, he's
  taken up gardening and works in the yard at least four hours
  every week.

Who has a balanced fitness program? Although less vigorous·
than Joe's (the weight lifter) or Sue's (the marathon runner), Jerry
has a balanced fitness program. His exercises include activities to
develop adequate levels of muscle strength and endurance, and
flexibility in addition to cardiovascular endurance.

A balanced fitness program should be a part of every person's
lifestyle. As you age, muscle strength and endurance, and flexibility may become as important as cardiovascular endurance to
quality of life. For this reason, the Institute for Aerobics Research
is currently conducting a five-year study, funded by the National
Institutes of Health, to investigate the long term effects of strength
and flexibility on health and function. This book brings you
practical results of research from this institute and other research
authorities that you can practice in your everyday life.

IT'S NEVER TOO LATE

Balanced fitness can do more to ensure a long, healthy and happy life than just about anything else known to medical science today. It's never too late to start a fitness program but ideally, you should build strong bones and muscles, flexibility and a strong cardiovascular system early in life and enter the later years with your physical potential at its maximum.

You can probably survive without much difficulty the early years of your life (birth to age 30) with relatively poor lifestyle behaviors -- bad eating habits and inactivity. Most people naturally have adequate fitness to meet the demands of these years. But by the time you're into the middle years, the aging process has set in and your body will begin to show the neglect, unless you take action to slow the decline in function.

It's surprising how soon the aging process begins for sedentary people:

* Aerobic fitness in sedentary people starts to decline in the early twenties.

* Flexibility starts to decline in the mid twenties.

* Bone strength declines starting in the mid thirties.

* Muscle strength declines after the late thirties or early forties.

* Skin elasticity declines after the early forties and wrinkles become more prominent.

Active men and women have a considerable fitness advantage when compared to sedentary individuals. The chart below shows results from the analysis of maximal treadmill test performance in more than 4,000 men examined at the Cooper Clinic. The active men have much higher fitness at any age. This advantage becomes more important with age, and active people can maintain a high level of function much later in life.

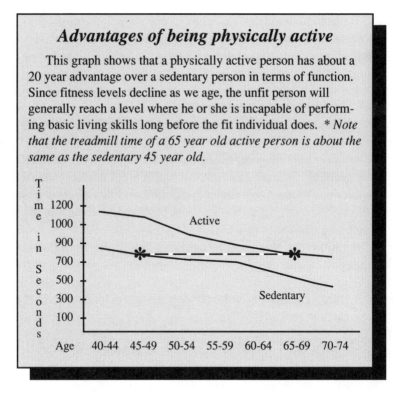

Advantages of being physically active

This graph shows that a physically active person has about a 20 year advantage over a sedentary person in terms of function. Since fitness levels decline as we age, the unfit person will generally reach a level where he or she is incapable of performing basic living skills long before the fit individual does. * *Note that the treadmill time of a 65 year old active person is about the same as the sedentary 45 year old.*

LIVING LONGER,
LIVING STRONGER

What would you like to be able to do at age 70 or even 85? You know, there's a good chance you'll live that long. If right now you're 50 years old and male, on the average you have 26 years of life ahead of you. If you're a woman, you have 31 years. That's nearly half of your adult life! Although the human lifespan isn't expected to increase significantly, it is predicted that a higher percentage of the people will live longer than ever before.

Expected life span

| | Year of Birth | | | |
| | 1940 | | 1950 | |
	Men	Women	Men	Women
Percentage Surviving Until Age:				
70 Years	46	55	50	65
80 Years	9	14	12	21

Certainly you agree that it would be ideal to live life to its fullest until the last possible moment. This concept is called "compressed morbidity." If death is not sudden, due to an accident or a heart attack, then there is usually a period of disease or disability that precedes death.

An important goal for us as individuals and as a society should be to maintain a high level of functional fitness for as long as possible, compressing the period of morbidity before death to a few days or weeks, rather than years -- which has been the case for too many people in the past. If this goal were realized, we would enjoy the benefits of a healthy and more productive work force and a reduction in the burden of health care costs to both the public and private sectors.

Compressed morbidity

This example shows theoretical aging curves for two individuals. The line labeled independent living indicates a threshold of function required for living independently. When a person's functional capability falls below this threshold, he or she must be institutionalized or receive custodial care. In this example, both people die at age 90. The sedentary person had to be institutionalized for the last 10 years of life, while the active person can live independently with adequate function until near the end of life.

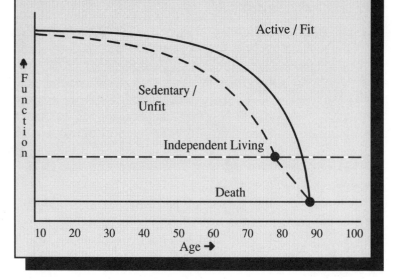

WHAT IS BALANCED FITNESS?

Traditionally, "fitness" has been solely a measure of aerobic (cardiovascular) endurance. And certainly, aerobic endurance is an essential component of health and quality of life. However, there are two other components that are nearly as important. It is only from appropriate fitness levels in all three components that you achieve balanced fitness, and thus optimal health and quality of life. These three components are:

* *Aerobic fitness (cardiovascular endurance)*

* *Flexibility*

* *Muscle strength and endurance.*

Coordination, balance, agility, speed, power and reaction time are also components of fitness, but they relate to efficiency of movement and athletic performance more than health.

AEROBIC FITNESS

Aerobic exercise is particularly beneficial for the cardiovascular system and aids in maintaining ideal body weight. Dr. Kenneth Cooper coined the term "aerobics" in the early 1960s as he was developing the physical fitness program for the U. S. Air Force. Today "aerobics" is a household word. It first appeared in the *Oxford English Dictionary* in 1986 defined as follows:

"A method of physical exercise for producing beneficial changes in the respiratory and circulatory systems by activities which require only a modest increase in oxygen intake and so can be maintained."

"Aerobic" without the "s" means with air or with oxygen. You can easily see the connection Dr. Cooper made between "aerobic" and "aerobics" in defining a type of exercise that benefits the systems that transport oxygen to the body: the heart, lungs and blood vessels. Examples of aerobic exercise include brisk walking, jogging, cycling, swimming, dancing, cross-country skiing and rowing.

To be sure that an exercise qualifies as "aerobics," ask the following questions:

* Does it use the large muscle groups of your body, such as buttocks, thighs and back?

* Does it raise your heart rate and can you continue the activity for more than a few minutes?

* Does it cause you to feel warm, perspire and breathe heavily without being really out of breath and without feeling any burning sensation in the muscles?

If you answered "yes" to all three questions, the activity is definitely aerobics.

FLEXIBILITY

Irving, a retired engineer and grandfather, came to the Cooper Clinic for a checkup and fitness evaluation. He reported that overall he was feeling great: running three miles every morning, eating well, spending a lot of time with his grandchildren, two or three fishing trips every summer in Canada. In all, life was very pleasant. It was too bad, he said, that his golf game was starting to suffer because of stiffness in his shoulders and upper back.

He mentioned his mother's arthritis to his physician wondering aloud if there was a connection. Upon examination of Irving's back, his doctor discovered the problem wasn't arthritis at all. The stiffness in his back was caused simply by lack of use and poor muscle tone. His doctor taught him a variety of stretching exercises to increase flexibility in his upper back. A strength training program was recommended to exercise specifically the muscles of the shoulders and upper back. The following year Irving visited the clinic for another evaluation. When asked about the stiffness, Irving reported he'd added 20 yards to his drive!

Flexibility is an essential component of balanced fitness. It can be defined as the ability to move a part of the body through its full range of motion. Other than bone and joint diseases, limitations to flexibility are primarily caused by tight muscles, ligaments and tendons -- all of which can be addressed with appropriate flexibility exercises.

Proper stretching can reduce muscle tension, improve ease of movement, help maintain good posture and increase range of motion. Yet, stretching exercises are often neglected. Many people consider the limbering-up process to be so obvious that they never learn to do it properly. They stretch too little, too much or at the wrong time.

Stretching can smooth the transition into all-out effort of aerobic activity or strength training. Thus, you should choose flexibility exercises compatible with the other exercise activities you are performing. If you are preparing to run, stretch the hamstrings, quads and calves. If you are preparing to lift weights, stretch the muscles you'll use during your lifts. A tennis player should develop flexibility in the shoulders and in abdominal muscles involved in the twisting motions demanded by the sport.

Descriptions and diagrams for flexibility exercises are provided in Part VI of this book.

MUSCLE STRENGTH AND ENDURANCE

Muscle strength and endurance may be as important as aerobic conditioning to the quality of your life and your overall physical and mental health. Starting the lawnmower, carrying the groceries, opening a stubborn jar lid, swinging the kids overhead, you notice the benefits of strong muscles in almost every aspect of day-to-day life. Strength training can also help protect against injury, maintain bone mass, control blood pressure and reduce body fat. And, just as important, strong muscles can improve your self-confidence and esteem.

Athletes who achieve high levels of performance and exercise physiologists who study them in the laboratory make a distinction between muscle strength and muscle endurance. Muscle strength is the maximum force that can be generated by a muscle or muscle group. People who have strong muscles can lift heavy objects, jump, pull, push, carry and do other activities more easily. Strong muscles, particularly in the back and abdomen, encourage good posture and can help prevent back pain, one of the most common complaints doctors hear.

The strength of any particular muscle is dependent upon its size and its ability to "recruit" muscle fibers to do the work. People generally have more muscle fibers available than they typically recruit for everyday activities. You've heard stories about individuals who have been able to exhibit extraordinary strength in an emergency situation, a fire or automobile accident, to save their own life or someone else's. These are examples of people recruiting more muscle fibers than normal.

Muscle endurance is the ability of the muscle to make repeated contractions with a less than maximal load, in contrast to muscle strength which is defined as one maximal effort. If you can lift a weight many times before becoming fatigued, you have good muscle endurance.

During the early and middle years of your life, the amount of muscle strength and endurance you need will be influenced by your occupation or recreational pursuits. It's difficult to pinpoint exactly the amount of muscle strength and endurance you need to help protect against the degenerative processes of inactivity. The American College of Sports Medicine recommends that healthy adults perform a minimum of 8 to 10 exercises involving the major muscle groups a minimum of two times per week. At least one *set* of 8 to 12 *repetitions* to near-fatigue should be completed during each session. These recommendations were based on two factors:

* Most people aren't likely to adhere to workout sessions that last more than 60 minutes. (The regimen outlined above can be completed in 30 minutes or less.)

* While more frequent and intense training is likely to build greater strength, the difference is usually relatively small.

BENEFITS OF BALANCED FITNESS

In a survey conducted by the Institute for Aerobics Research in 1990, over 1,000 adults were asked to tell why they believe regular exercise is important. Here's what they said, beginning with the most common response:

	MEN	WOMEN
-To improve health	83%	79%
-To get more physically fit	70%	79%
-To improve appearance	58%	75%
-To prevent a heart attack	58%	49%
-To maintain a desirable weight	54%	58%
-To lose weight	52%	66%
-To reduce the effects of stress	51%	60%
-To improve self-esteem	48%	61%
-To relax	41%	48%
-To get stronger	36%	27%
-To have fun	35%	29%
-To prevent muscle/joint problems	33%	36%
-To socialize	11%	11%

Obviously, people think there are many good reasons to exercise. Yet, a large portion of the adult population remains sedentary. The facts about the benefits of balanced fitness, particularly about strength training, should help you start or continue your exercise program.

HEART HEALTH

The list of benefits to the cardiovascular and respiratory systems that result from balanced fitness is impressive:

*Improved cholesterol profile to include higher HDL ("good") cholesterol and lower LDL ("bad") cholesterol and triglyceride levels.

*Increased volume and strength of the ventricles (lower chambers of the heart).

*Increased heart stroke volume (the volume of blood the heart pumps with each contraction).

*Decreased heart rate at rest and during moderate exercise.

*Increased blood delivery to the active muscles during exercise.

*Increased blood volume and total hemoglobin (the oxygen-carrying component of red blood cells).

*Increased number of capillaries in the skeletal muscles.

*More efficient oxygen supply to and waste removal from the muscles.

*More effective use of oxygen in the muscle cells.

*Increased respiratory muscle strength including diaphragm and abdominals.

In addition, several studies have reported that regular aerobic exercise can be effective in preventing and treating mild or moderate forms of *hypertension* (high blood pressure).

Fitness and mortality

The Aerobics Center Longitudinal Study, conducted by the Institute for Aerobics Research and published in the *Journal of the American Medical Association* (November 3, 1989), followed 13,344 men and women over eight years. Fitness levels were measured by treadmill performance and subjects were assigned to five fitness categories, ranging from low to high according to their treadmill times.

* Death rates from all causes for the least-fit men were 3.4 times higher than the most-fit men and for the least-fit women, 4.6 times higher than the most-fit women.

* Higher levels of physical fitness were beneficial even in those with other risk factors such as high blood pressure, elevated cholesterol, cigarette smoking and family history of heart disease. For example, it's better not to smoke; but fit smokers are less likely to die prematurely than unfit smokers. In fact, unfit people without these risk factors had higher death rates than fit people with them.

* Cancer death rates were significantly lower in physically fit men and women.

Even moderate levels of exercise will result in a fitness level associated with a greatly reduced risk of premature death. Just getting out of the least-fit category and into the moderate-fitness category provides substantial benefits.

LOSE BODY FAT AND KEEP IT OFF

Being overweight, or more specifically over fat, is a serious health problem in the country today. The U.S. Surgeon General estimates that 20-25% of American adults have too much body fat for optimal health.

Body composition describes the makeup of the body in terms of *lean body mass* and *body fat*. Lean body mass consists of muscles, bone, nerve tissue, skin and organs of the body. These are the active parts of the body. Body fat is a tissue that stores energy for future use.

As a measure of health and fitness, body composition is more important than body weight. To illustrate this point, consider the running back playing professional football who requires a great deal of muscle strength for his position. Because muscle is heavier than fat per unit volume, at 5' 10" tall and a weight of 200 lbs. he appears to be overweight according to a standard height-weight chart. But he's not over fat. In fact, his percentage of body fat is very low, roughly eight to ten percent. Healthy adult men typically have approximately 21% body fat and healthy adult women have approximately 27% body fat.

In considering the health implications of excess body fat, it is important to note where fat is deposited on the body. There is scientific evidence that suggests that deposits of fat in the trunk of the body, as opposed to an even distribution of fat in the arms, trunk and legs, put people at higher risk for certain diseases, including cardiovascular disease and type II diabetes. Unfortunately, where you store fat when gaining weight and where you lose fat during weight loss may be to a large extent genetically determined.

Aerobic exercise is an important part of fat control because it reduces feelings of hunger, decreases fat storage and increases fat *metabolism*. Aerobic exercise increases the metabolic rate during the activity and may keep it elevated for some time afterwards.

Reducing caloric intake alone isn't the answer to controlling fat. Dieting without exercise results in a loss of lean body mass as well as fat and causes the body's metabolism to slow so that the body can more efficiently use the reduced number of calories it's receiving. As your metabolic rate decreases, you'll have to eat less and less to continue losing weight. Then when you stop dieting, the weight usually returns rapidly because the metabolism takes a while to readjust and the lean body mass lost with diet alone can't be quickly replaced. This is often referred to as the "yo-yo" effect -- repeatedly losing and gaining weight. There is evidence that this pattern creates a greater health risk than remaining at a constant weight.

Reducing caloric intake while maintaining a regular program of aerobic exercise helps maintain muscle mass and produces a reduction in fat tissue. Strength training, an integral part of balanced fitness, may play an important role in fat control because increasing the amount of muscle in the body may cause an increase in the basal metabolic rate and an associated increase in calorie expenditure.

Losing fat, toning muscle and increasing muscle strength also has positive benefits in terms of appearance, posture, attitude and self-concept. You'll look better and feel better about yourself!

CONTROL STRESS

Balanced fitness provides psychological as well as physiological benefits. Indeed, most people today accept the mind-body connection and understand the importance of physical fitness to emotional well-being.

In recent years, there has been a great deal published in medical literature and the popular press on the effects of stress. Essentially, stress is a physiological reaction to a psychological event. It's best explained in terms of cause and effect. The cause, or stressor, is a demand that disrupts your sense of calm or balance and initiates the stress response, or effect. The response consists of physiological changes within the body that prepare you to "fight or flee." In primitive humans, this innate response helped them to fight or flee from danger and therefore to survive. In modern man, these same responses occur, but in most situations, the response is not necessary for survival and the hormones then become harmful by-products.

Clearly, not all stress is bad. Some stress is good and necessary for productivity and growth. There are, however, symptoms or behaviors that have been associated with stress-related illnesses or diseases. A few of these include:

-Anxiety	-Depression
-Insomnia	-Unexplained pain
-Migraine headaches	-Indigestion
-Skipped or irregular	-Skin eruptions
menstrual cycles	-Eating disorders
-Teeth grinding	-Sexual dysfunction

If you're under undue stress, you may be unable to perform daily tasks as well as usual, or be insensitive to others, or show explosive anger in response to minor irritations.

Since the natural release when feeling stressed is body movement, exercise can be an effective stress management tool, particularly if the activity isn't overly competitive.

After a vigorous workout, the muscles are tired. You feel relaxed. This tranquil feeling of well-being has been linked to chemicals called endorphins. Endorphins are strong, natural pain killers that are produced by the body and released during exercise. They remain in the bloodstream for hours. Dr. Cooper calls aerobic exercise "nature's best tranquilizer."

STRONG AND HEALTHY BONES

As you get older, your bones lose minerals and become gradually weaker and more brittle, and the potential for fracture increases. This condition is called *osteoporosis* and is especially a problem for women after menopause because of loss of estrogen. Men don't usually have this condition until later.

Women who have any of these characteristics may be at particular risk for osteoporosis:

-Sedentary lifestyle
-Family history of osteoporosis
-Light frame
-Fair skin and hair
-Low calcium intake
-Complete hysterectomy (without estrogen replacement therapy)
-Cigarette smoking
-High protein intake
-Childlessness
-High caffeine intake
-High alcohol intake

Research has indicated that stronger bones may result from physical activity, especially weight-bearing exercise, although the exact forms and levels of physical activity necessary to control osteoporosis are not yet known. In general, people who have exercised regularly throughout their lives are likely to have greater bone mass and thus less risk of fracture in the later years than those who have been inactive.

Bones, like muscles, respond to the overload principle -- they get stronger and thicker the more they are used or exercised. Professional tennis players, for example, often have thicker and stronger bones in the "playing arm" than in their other arm. Weight lifters tend to have thicker arm bones than runners. Even swimming, best known for its excellent cardiovascular benefits, is believed to provide some protection against weak bones.

Building high bone mass early in life (teens to mid thirties) through diet and exercise is important, especially for women. To maintain a healthy musculoskeletal system, particularly after age 40 or 50, women and men should adopt a balanced fitness program that stresses the areas at risk for fracture (hips, wrists, low spine) with activities such as calisthenics, strength training, aerobic dance, walking, jogging and cross-country skiing. In addition to regular exercise, sufficient amounts of calcium and vitamin D in the diet are important. Many post-menopausal women are also given estrogen replacement prescriptions by their physicians. There is no consensus on this issue, though you should ask your doctor about estrogen therapy if you're past menopause.

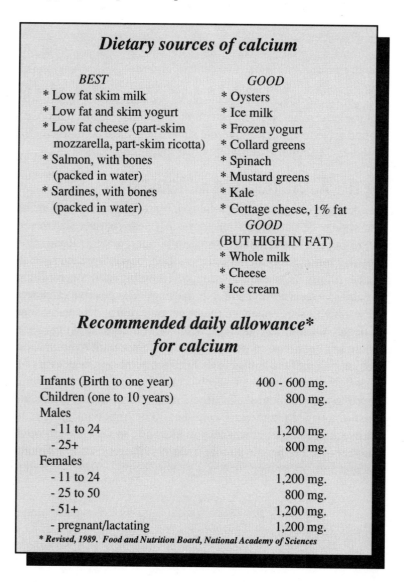

Dietary sources of calcium

BEST	GOOD
* Low fat skim milk	* Oysters
* Low fat and skim yogurt	* Ice milk
* Low fat cheese (part-skim	* Frozen yogurt
mozzarella, part-skim ricotta)	* Collard greens
* Salmon, with bones	* Spinach
(packed in water)	* Mustard greens
* Sardines, with bones	* Kale
(packed in water)	* Cottage cheese, 1% fat

GOOD
(BUT HIGH IN FAT)
* Whole milk
* Cheese
* Ice cream

*Recommended daily allowance**
for calcium

Infants (Birth to one year)	400 - 600 mg.
Children (one to 10 years)	800 mg.
Males	
- 11 to 24	1,200 mg.
- 25+	800 mg.
Females	
- 11 to 24	1,200 mg.
- 25 to 50	800 mg.
- 51+	1,200 mg.
- pregnant/lactating	1,200 mg.

* Revised, 1989. Food and Nutrition Board, National Academy of Sciences

MYTHS ABOUT EXERCISE

Unfortunately, many people make decisions about why or why not to exercise based on incorrect information. For this reason, it's important to recognize and refute some of the most common myths about exercise, particularly about strength training.

MYTH: ALL IT TAKES IS AEROBICS

Aerobic exercise is essential to overall health and well-being and should be the foundation of your fitness routine. However, flexibility and strength training are important, as well. Remember that the concept of balanced fitness goes beyond aerobics. Balanced fitness is obtained through a combination of aerobics, flexibility exercises and strength training. The positive effects of these activities are enhanced by proper nutrition and the avoidance of negative health and lifestyle behaviors such as smoking.

In talking about aerobic exercise, it's important to emphasize that jogging isn't the only aerobic exercise or the only way to get fit. There are many excellent aerobic exercises you can perform to improve your cardiovascular fitness level. Walking, bicycling and cross-country skiing are all excellent. The important thing is to choose an aerobic exercise that you like and can stick with through the years. Many people choose a variety of exercises to maintain interest and enjoyment.

MYTH: GET FIT IN JUST 10 MINUTES A WEEK

Your exercise time should be enjoyable -- a special time to do something for yourself. But many people say they can't find the time. Twenty to 30 minutes of aerobic activity three to five times per week is recommended to develop and maintain cardiovascular fitness. Strength and flexibility training require additional time. However, a recent study suggests that you may be able to divide your daily 20 to 30 minute workout into two or three 10 minute workouts and get almost the same effect as if you had done one 30 minute exercise session.

Some people think they have an adequate fitness program because they play a competitive sport, like softball or basketball, once a week. This type of exercise program won't provide accept-able results and is likely to place excessive stress on the cardiovas-cular and musculoskeletal systems. Get in shape to play the sport, don't play the sport to get in shape.

While it isn't possible to achieve and maintain fitness with only a few minutes of exercise a week (as some gimmicks would have you believe) you don't have to run marathons or spend hours in the weight room to get positive health benefits from exercise. Just getting out of the least-fit category into the moderate-fitness category provides substantial benefits.

MYTH: JUST EXERCISE THE FAT SPOTS

Spot reducing is a myth. You can't exercise one part of the body to reduce fat in just that area. Fat "comes off" all over and "goes on" all over. The specific locations where fat comes off during weight loss is genetically determined.

There is no conclusive scientific evidence that anything but regular exercise and a lower calorie diet will cause a natural reduction in stored body fat, including those deposits that are localized. The amount of fat that "comes off" depends upon the number of calories burned. Using passive exercise machines that do the work for you have never been proven to be of any value in controlling weight or improving cardiovascular fitness. There are surgical techniques that remove fat in specific areas (liposuction) but these methods are not recommended and the likelihood of the fat returning is high.

A study using male volunteers investigated the effect of a training program that focused on fat deposited in the abdomen. At the beginning of the study, biopsies were performed to analyze fat cells from the abdomen as well as from the arms, legs, and upper back. The subjects participated in a 27-day sit-up program during which they performed over 5,000 sit-ups. Biopsies were repeated in the same areas at the end of the training program and fat cells were compared. If spot reducing were possible, you'd expect the fat cells in the abdomen to shrink and the size of the cells in the other sites to remain the same. This didn't happen. Fat cells in all sites decreased in size, confirming that fat loss is overall rather than specific to one area of the body.

You can do spot-firming exercises. For example, if you concentrate on doing leg presses to firm your thighs and buttocks, over time you will notice that they appear firmer, though the fat is still there. You've increased muscle rather than decreased fat.

MYTH: LACK OF EXERCISE TURNS MUSCLE TO FAT

Inactivity may cause your muscles to shrink and may cause more fat to be deposited, but muscle doesn't turn to fat. Muscle and fat are different types of tissue. Fat could replace the muscle so that your arm or waist is the same size, but the composition would be different. In fact, when you start to get out of shape, you may notice a change in appearance before a change in weight.

MYTH: EXERCISE TURNS FAT TO MUSCLE

In the same way lack of exercise doesn't turn muscle to fat, exercise doesn't turn fat to muscle. These are two different types of tissue. However, by creating a calorie deficit, strength training may contribute to fat loss. Toning and firming muscle with strength training can also improve appearance, although this doesn't necessarily mean you've lost fat. But definitely, the fat won't turn to muscle.

MYTH: NO PAIN, NO GAIN

You don't have to hurt to get the benefits of exercise. If you want to lose fat, increase your cardiovascular fitness, improve muscle strength and endurance, and improve flexibility, then take it easy and build up slowly. You may experience some stiffness and soreness when you first begin your exercise program, but it should disappear as you grow more accustomed to your routine.

Remember, exercise should be enjoyable. No one is likely to continue an exercise program that hurts. And, recognize that the discomfort of a fatigued muscle is different than the sharp pain that comes from a muscle tear or a ligament strain. Pain that warns of possible injury should be avoided.

MYTH: STRENGTH TRAINING IS A MAN'S SPORT

The idea that only males need to be concerned with their strength is ludicrous. Both men and women need and can enjoy the benefits of strength training including improvements in body composition, increased resting metabolism through the addition of muscle, improved self-concept, prevention of low back problems and joint injury, stronger bones and perhaps the delay of osteoporosis (especially significant for women) and possibly beneficial changes in cholesterol and blood pressure levels.

MYTH: WOMEN DEVELOP BIG, BULGING MUSCLES

Although women can become very strong through strength training, they won't normally develop the bulging muscles that some men develop. This is partly because they have less *testosterone*, the male hormone, in their bodies. Women produce testosterone at a rate of one-tenth to one-twentieth of that of males. Combined with heavy lifting, genetics and several other factors, testosterone helps make men's muscles big.

That said, some female athletes do develop large muscle mass. This may be related to genetics or because they are producing above-average levels of testosterone. Or they might be taking steroids which can produce the same effect.

MYTH: STRENGTH TRAINING MAKES YOU MUSCLE-BOUND

Many people believe strength training causes tight, bulky muscles that prevent you from moving freely. This condition is frequently referred to as being "muscle-bound." Most people who become muscle-bound have trained improperly developing certain muscles while neglecting others.

To avoid becoming muscle-bound, work all major muscle groups, exercise the joints through the full range of motion and include flexibility exercises for balanced fitness. If you don't perform stretching exercises, you can lose flexibility as you age. The flexibility of a weight lifter is not inherently worse than that of a marathon runner, but both need to stretch.

MYTH: VITAMINS AND SUPPLEMENTS -- THE PERFORMANCE EDGE

Vitamins do not provide energy, nor do they build body tissue. If you eat a balanced diet of adequate calories, you shouldn't need supplemental vitamins. In fact, a comprehensive study by the government of over 1,400 dietary supplements found that none provided an added benefit above a balanced diet.

But does taking vitamins involve any risks? Yes. Even some of the water-soluble vitamins, such as C, B-6 and niacin, in high doses can be toxic. If overdosages of fat-soluble vitamins are taken, especially vitamins A and D, the results could be serious, even fatal. These vitamins are stored in fat tissue and overly large quantities can interfere with normal body functions.

The need for other nutritional supplements while participating in an exercise program, particularly strength training, is a frequent topic of debate. Protein requirements are somewhat greater when you're attempting to build muscle, but not to the extent that the public has been led to believe. Most of us get an amount of protein in our diet that is sufficient for even the most strenuous strength training program.

Salt tablets are no longer recommended, either. In fact, salt tablets can be harmful, contributing to dehydration and irritating the stomach. Water for hydration and complex carbohydrates for energy are the components of the diet that should be emphasized as part of an exercise program. Women may benefit from an iron and calcium supplement.

Some people take anabolic steroids to enhance their performance. These drugs are similar in their muscle-building characteristics to testosterone, the male sex hormone. Steroids are a very serious health hazard and are illegal when used for the purpose of athletic enhancement. **Steroids have no place in any fitness program.**

MYTH: STRENGTH TRAINING LEADS TO HIGH BLOOD PRESSURE

Traditionally, people with high blood pressure have been discouraged from performing any form of strength training because of the perceived risk of heart attack or stroke. It's true that your blood pressure increases during strength training, but recent studies that have investigated long term effects of strength training and resting blood pressure have failed to show any negative effect. In fact, some of these studies indicate that strength training can decrease resting blood pressure.

However, *isometric* exercises are generally not recommended for people with high blood pressure. *Isotonic* and *isokinetic* exercises are very effective and create less risk for the exerciser. **If you have high blood pressure, check with your doctor before beginning any exercise program.**

MYTH: STRENGTH TRAINING CAUSES ARTHRITIS AND OTHER JOINT DISEASES

Osteoarthritis is a degenerative disease in which the cartilage lining the bony surfaces inside the joint becomes progressively thinner until the bone beneath the cartilage on both sides of the joint ultimately becomes exposed. In the advanced stages of osteoarthritis, the exposed bones rub against each other causing pain and severely limited joint movement.

There is no scientific evidence that exercise of any kind causes osteoarthritis in people whose joints were normal when they started exercising. People who do develop osteoarthritis may have had previous joint injuries or surgery. Former athletes are likely to have had injuries from sports such as football, rugby, soccer or basketball.

MYTH: STRENGTH TRAINING IS A YOUNG PERSON'S SPORT

Everyone can benefit from strength training. Older people who have become too weak to carry out daily tasks are precisely the group that can benefit the most from strength training! There is a difference in the type and degree of response that is related to age, but the notion that only the young need strength training is incorrect. Strength training can improve function and quality of life at any age.

Because your ability to add muscle mass and strength decreases after about age fifty, it is best to be well-conditioned before the later years so that you'll be able to perform better and longer. However, a recent study shows some amazing gains in strength and muscle mass from strength training even among people in their nineties.

PART II

HOW YOUR MUSCLES WORK

ANATOMY OF A MUSCLE

You have three types of muscle tissues in your body, each with a separate function. These are cardiac, the *involuntary muscle* of the heart; smooth, the involuntary muscles of the digestive system, blood vessels and others; and skeletal, the *voluntary* muscles of the body which are those under your control.

The skeletal system is your body's support structure. It's made up of bones and joints. Each type of joint is designed for a specific movement. Your shoulders and hips, for example, have ball-and-socket joints, in which the ball-like head of one bone fits into the socket of another, enabling you to move your arms and legs in all directions. The hinge joints of your elbows, fingers, toes and knees open and close like the hinges of a door. Vertebral joints connect the vertebrae of your spine. Each vertebra has only limited motion -- however, as a unit, your spine can move in all directions.

The skeletal muscles are attached to the bones by means of tendons. Ligaments attach bones to other bones. Joint cartilage protects the bones from wear and provides smooth, moist surfaces that permit joint movement with a minimum of friction.

To control the voluntary muscles, your brain receives and sends messages through your spinal cord to the nerves connected to muscles. These signals tell the muscles when to go into action, how strongly they should contract, and how many muscles are needed to execute the movement. The muscles send signals back to your brain, telling it what has occurred. With this information, your brain can make adjustments, if needed, to allow you to perform the activity as you desire.

This process occurs constantly, when you run, walk, lift or hold an object, dance, play the piano or perform countless other tasks and activities. Whether the movements are job-related, recreational, athletic, rhythmical or related to daily living, all require the contraction and relaxation of specific muscles.

Did you know?

* The human body has over 600 muscles containing more than 6 billion microscopic muscle fibers. Each fiber is so strong that it can support more than 1,000 times its own weight.

* The skeletal muscles make up from 40 to 50 percent of total body weight.

* The production of voluntary movements by skeletal muscle is one of the most essential activities of the body.

* You have approximately the same number of muscle fibers in your body now as when you were an infant. Of course, as you grew from a child to an adult, the fibers grew bigger and stronger, but the total number probably hasn't changed much at all, if any.

MUSCLE FIBERS

All skeletal muscle is composed of two major types of fibers: *slow-twitch* (red) and *fast-twitch* (white). The relative number of slow-twitch and fast-twitch fibers is related to the muscle's job. The total number of fibers doesn't change much and red fibers always remain red and white fibers always remain white. The ratio of red to white fibers is set genetically and doesn't change in response to training. The endurance and/or strength of a given muscle depends upon the distribution of the fibers the muscle is made of and the blood supply to the muscle.

There are marked differences in function between slow-twitch and fast-twitch fibers. As the name indicates, slow-twitch muscle fibers contract at a slow rate. These fibers function predominantly "aerobically" using oxygen directly from the blood and are slow to fatigue. For activities that require less than maximal force, like riding a bicycle or jogging, slow-twitch muscle fibers bear the major burden because they provide the steady source of energy that these activities require.

Fast-twitch fibers contract at a fast rate. Energy is released to white fibers by predominantly anaerobic processes. Muscles composed mainly of fast-twitch fibers have great strength, but they have less endurance. White fibers are larger, contract with more force, and are well-equipped for short duration, high intensity work such as weight lifting or sprinting, although with aerobic training, fast-twitch fibers can improve their endurance capacity.

There is actually a third group of fibers called intermediate fibers which have characteristics of both slow- and fast-twitch fibers. Muscles containing intermediate fibers have strength as well as endurance and are most likely to adapt to a fitness training program.

The only way to know what kinds of fibers you have in a specific muscle is through muscle biopsies which, of course, are not recommended or necessary for the person who exercises for health reasons. Generally, world class aerobic athletes (marathon runners, cyclists, cross-country skiers, etc.) have more slow-twitch (red) muscle fibers, while world class power or anaerobic event athletes (shot putters, power lifters, sprinters) have more fast-twitch (white) muscle fibers than normal individuals.

Regardless what your ratio of red to white fibers is, you can participate successfully in both anaerobic and aerobic activities. Remember that for the purpose of balanced fitness, success is defined as the amount of enjoyment and satisfaction that you derive from all aspects of your life, not in developing proficiency in a particular activity.

PROPERTIES OF MUSCLE TISSUE

CONTRACTIONS

Muscle tissue is unique in its ability to contract and relax on command from the nervous system. Like an elastic band, a muscle can be stretched then return to its resting length when the stretching force is removed. For this reason, muscles are said to have the properties of elasticity and extensibility.

Unlike an elastic band, a muscle can also be shortened beyond its normal resting length by pulling from both ends toward the center. This property is called contraction and results in a muscle that is shorter and greater in circumference. The average muscle fiber can be shortened to approximately one-half and stretched to one and one-half times its resting length.

A limb moves when the muscles receive an electrochemical signal from the nervous system, which causes one muscle group, the *agonist*, to contract while the opposite group, the *antagonist*, relaxes or blocks movement. The limb then pivots on whatever joint is involved.

When contracting, muscle fibers follow an "all or none" principle. In other words, each fiber is either "off" or "on." There's no half-throttle. If you need to contract a muscle slowly, say at half speed, then only a portion of the fibers within the muscle are recruited to do the work and the contraction is weak. If you need a strong contraction to lift a heavy object, then many fibers are recruited. One result of strength training is that it may enable you to recruit more muscle fibers.

METABOLISM

Metabolism is the sum of all the chemical processes that occur in the entire body. It is the means by which energy (calories) from primarily fats and carbohydrates is made available and used to fuel basic body processes. Metabolism takes place continuously in all of the organs throughout the body. Resting or basal metabolic rate is the amount of energy your body uses while you are at complete rest during a specified period of time.

During exercise, the activity of the muscles needs energy over and above the amount required for basal metabolism. The amounts of fats and carbohydrates that are used to fuel muscle contractions vary depending on the amount of oxygen that is supplied to the working muscles. While the metabolism of carbohydrates does not require oxygen, the breakdown of fats for energy does. Also, the body has a limited amount of stored carbohydrate; stored fat is a concentrated and near limitless source of energy.

Very little oxygen is provided to the working muscles during vigorous, all-out types of exercises, such as sprinting or weight lifting. In *anaerobic* exercises like these, carbohydrates are the major fuel source. Also, lactic acid, a by-product of carbohydrate metabolism during anaerobic exercise, is produced. Lactic acid causes muscle fatigue. Thus, because of lactic acid build-up and the limited supply of carbohydrates in the body, anaerobic activities can't be sustained for a long period of time.

Aerobic exercise on the other hand, requires oxygen in order for the body to produce energy for the working muscles. The energy needed during aerobic exercise comes from both fats and carbohydrates. Although some lactic acid is produced during aerobic exercise, it remains in the normal range. As long as oxygen is provided, exercise can be maintained for a long time.

Did you know?

* As muscles work, causing the body to move, they produce much of the heat that keeps you warm.

HYPERTROPHY

Muscles have the unique ability to grow larger and stronger. *Hypertrophy* is the increase in the size of the muscle caused by an increase in the thickness of the individual muscle fibers.

There are tremendous individual differences in the adaptation of muscles to training. In general, because the male sex hormone, testosterone, stimulates the protein-synthesizing mechanisms responsible for muscle growth, men demonstrate greater hypertrophy than women. Men also have more muscle fibers and their fibers are larger initially than those of women.

The fastest gains in muscle size are usually seen in those muscles which in everyday life do the least work in relation to their genetic potential. This partially explains why a person who has been hospitalized for a long period of time and may be suffering from some muscle loss *(atrophy)* can make significant gains. Muscle hypertrophy depends both on the severity of the overload, and the total duration of the overload. Although most of the increase in muscle size that occurs with strength training results from hypertrophy, there is now evidence that muscle size can also increase due to fiber splitting, which is called hyperplasia.

MUSCLE SORENESS

There are two types of muscle soreness that you're likely to experience due to strength training: acute soreness (during exercise) and delayed soreness. Acute soreness can also mean injury.

The delayed soreness you feel 24 to 72 hours after strenuous exercise isn't fully understood. Possible explanations for this discomfort include torn tissues, muscle spasms and damage to connective tissue. Of these possibilities, the latter appears most likely. Because muscle pain receptors are most concentrated around the tendons and connective tissue, you often feel the discomfort where the muscle joins the tendon. Though in cases of severe soreness, the pain may be generalized throughout the muscle.

Delayed muscle soreness is most likely to occur when you're just beginning to exercise (if you've been previously sedentary) or if you're increasing the intensity of your workout too quickly. Muscle soreness may vary from slight stiffness that disappears rapidly to severe pain that reduces flexibility and interferes with mobility.

A popular misconception about delayed soreness is that it's caused by the build up of lactic acid. This isn't true. Lactic acid is removed from the muscles within an hour or so after the end of exercise. Also, some activities that are known to produce lactic acid don't cause soreness and other activities cause soreness when no lactic acid is present.

Muscles can rupture or tear if they are put under great or sudden strain. If muscle pain is severe or persists longer than a few days, you should see a physician, as you should with any muscle injury that causes deformation, swelling or inflammation.

PRINCIPLES OF STRENGTH TRAINING

The principles discussed below apply to all types of exercises: aerobic, strength, and flexibility. These principles are especially important in the development or improvement phase of your program.

OVERLOAD

Muscles grow stronger in response to *overload* or stress. Overload may be accomplished in one of four ways:

* increasing resistance

* increasing repetitions

* decreasing rest time between sets

* increasing the number of training sessions per week.

To develop maximal strength, you should perform few repetitions (4 to 6) with heavy resistance. To develop maximal endurance, you should perform 20 to 30 repetitions with light to moderate resistance. A compromise will yield both strength and endurance. Most people find that 8 to 12 repetitions per exercise provides ideal results. To determine whether you are overloading a muscle optimally, ensure that the last repetition in each set is at near-maximum effort. This isn't to say that you must perform at near-maximum effort to receive a benefit in terms of muscle endurance.

PROGRESSION

If a muscle is always worked at the same amount of *resistance*, it will maintain the same strength. When an exercise begins to feel easy, in other words you can perform two to three more repetitions than your original goal, you should increase the resistance. Progress gradually over a period of time to get the best improvement in muscle strength and endurance. You risk injury if you add resistance too soon.

When you reach a level of muscle strength and endurance that is satisfactory for your needs, you should initiate a maintenance program to preserve the gains that you've worked so hard to make. Generally, two workouts per week are sufficient for maintenance.

Remember that the principles of overload and *progression* apply to cardiovascular endurance, as well. In jogging, for example, overload is applied by increasing the distance or decreasing the time required to cover the distance. Heart rate can be used as an index of intensity for applying overload with aerobic conditioning.

Tips to remember in applying overload and progression

* Be patient.

* Improvements occur in small increments, but normally the greatest gains occur during the first six to eight weeks of an exercise program.

* Overload should be increased only when it becomes "easy" to perform the amount of work that you have been doing. Then you're ready to accept a new challenge.

SPECIFICITY

Your body adapts to demands imposed on it in highly specific ways. You must exercise the specific muscles you expect to develop. Leg exercises develop the legs and arm exercises develop the arms. For best results, attempt to isolate the muscles you are working. In other words, make them work without the assistance of other unneeded muscles.

The principle of *specificity* is extremely important for competitive athletes working to maximize their training results for a specific activity. In the same way, you can use the principle of specificity to improve your golf swing, your tennis backhand or swimming stroke.

But if your purpose is health and balanced fitness, you don't have to exercise under such constraints. You can vary your exercise activities to add interest and variety or to accommodate weather conditions, availability of equipment and facilities, or social considerations.

Case study

A track and field coach had two excellent prospects for the shot put event. Each athlete followed a training regimen that included alternating days of strength training and technique work. Bill weighed more and could bench press 75 pounds more than Steve. The overall technique and quickness of the two athletes appeared to be the same, so the coach was puzzled that Steve consistently performed better. The answer became apparent when the coach learned that Steve's strength training program consisted of incline presses which more closely simulates the shot put movement. Bill worked primarily on bench presses and was stronger in that particular movement. Steve, the athlete who trained with a high degree of specificity was more successful.

MUSCLE BALANCE

If left to its own resources, the body favors selected muscle groups. One muscle or muscle group naturally remains stronger while another remains weaker. Lack of balance between muscle groups can affect your posture, movement and even increase your risk of injury.

There are more than 430 skeletal muscles that appear in pairs on opposite sides of the joints of the body. Fewer than 80 pairs are responsible for the common vigorous movements you make during exercise. At any time, any particular muscle or muscle group can function in the role of either agonist or antagonist.

The rule of thumb when correcting muscle imbalance is to stretch the muscles that are stronger (see Figure II. 1) and to strengthen muscles that are weaker (see Figure II. 2). One exercise can often accomplish both purposes.

Example: Stretch the Quadricep and Strengthen the Hamstrings

Figure II. 1. *Quadricep Stretch.*
To stretch the quadriceps, raise the heel towards the buttocks and hold it there for at least 20 seconds. Repeat the process with the other leg.

Figure II. 2. *Leg Curl.*
To strengthen the hamstrings, raise the heel 8-12 repetitions for one or two sets toward the buttocks, preferably with resistance.

Pain and injury can occur when there is a lack of balance between the muscles supporting a joint, particularly in the weight-bearing joints. For example, strong hamstrings help stabilize the knee and protect it from injury. But without strong quadriceps, calf muscles, abductor/adductor muscles, tendons, ligaments and other structures to balance it, the joint is still at risk. In helping to stabilize and protect the joint, strong muscles can also limit the amount of damage done in the event of an injury and help speed recovery.

Muscle balance is also important in maintaining good posture. One of the most widespread health problems in the United States today is low back pain. Lumbar lordosis (swayback), although not the only cause of low back pain, is a frequent culprit. This is caused typically by strong, tight hip flexors and lower back muscles which force the pelvis to tilt forward. Over time, this forward rotation becomes worse when weak abdominals offer little resistance to the pull of the stronger muscles. Tight hamstrings can also contribute to swayback. Strengthening the abdominals and improving flexibility in the lower back, hamstrings and hip flexors will both improve posture and relieve this type of low back pain.

COMMON MUSCLE IMBALANCES

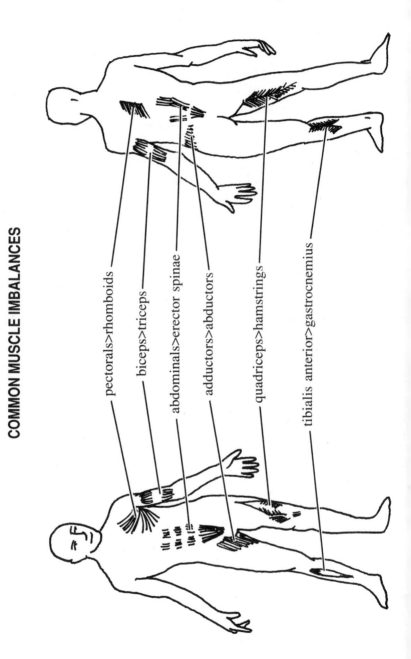

pectorals>rhomboids

biceps>triceps

abdominals>erector spinae

adductors>abductors

quadriceps>hamstrings

tibialis anterior>gastrocnemius

The **"Common Muscle Imbalances"** chart on page 44 lists muscle pairs commonly out of balance. Following are recommended exercises for achieving balance.

AGONIST/ANTAGONIST MUSCLE GROUPS

* Stronger > Weaker   *Recommended Action*

* Gastrocnemius > Tibialis Anterior
(Back of lower leg) (Front of lower leg)

STRETCH THE GASTROCNEMIUS: In a standing lunge with both feet pointed forward, straighten the rear leg to cause a stretch.

STRENGTHEN THE TIBIALIS ANTERIOR: Lift the toe toward the shin. Add resistance to gain more strength -- weights, rubber bands, partner-provided resistance.

* Quadriceps > Hamstrings
(Front of thigh) (Back of thigh)

STRETCH THE QUADRICEPS: Lie on the floor face down and lift the heel of one leg toward the buttocks. Grasp the ankle with either hand. Gently pull the heel out and back until the stretch is felt.

STRENGTHEN THE HAMSTRING: Lie on the floor face down and lift the heel of one leg toward the buttocks against resistance-- use weights, rubber bands, one leg against the other (cross at ankles), partner-provided resistance, furniture (isometric).

* Adductors > Abductors
(Inner thigh) (Outer thigh)

STRETCH THE ADDUCTORS: In a straddle sitting position, lean forward into the stretch from the hips.

STRENGTHEN THE ABDUCTORS: Lie on one side with the head resting on the hand. Lift the top leg to work the outer thigh. Repeat with other leg. As strength increases, add resistance: weights, rubber bands, partner-provided resistance.

* Erector Spinae > Abdominals
  (Lower back)   (Lower stomach)

STRETCH THE ERECTOR SPINAE: In a sitting position with the legs extended, slowly flex the trunk forward from the hips.

STRENGTHEN THE ABDOMINALS: Lie on the floor face up, knees bent. Curl the head and shoulders off the floor approximately 35 degrees. Keep knees bent while lifting up.

* Pectorals > Rhomboids
  (Chest)   (Upper back)

STRETCH THE PECTORALS: Face into a corner and stand about two feet away. Place one hand on each wall and slowly press into the corner until a stretch is felt.

STRENGTHEN THE RHOMBOIDS: Raise the arms to shoulder level and bend the elbows. Press the arms backward to stress the rhomboids. Use weights, if possible.

* Biceps > Triceps

STRETCH THE BICEPS: Generally, lack of bicep flexibility isn't a problem.

STRENGTHEN THE TRICEPS: After the elbow has been flexed, extend the arm to stress the tricep. The triceps can be overloaded by using body weight (push-ups or chair-dips) or by using hand weights or heavy resistance.

* The muscles identified as "stronger > weaker" are primarily responsible for these movements but are by no means the only muscles involved. There may be 10 or more additional muscles acting to assist in the movement.

TYPES OF STRENGTH TRAINING EXERCISES

ISOMETRIC EXERCISE

In the 1950s, this type of routine was hailed as the "quick and easy" way to enhance muscle strength. Further research has shown that isometric strength training is not without drawbacks.

Isometric strength is usually developed through muscle contractions against a stationary object or body part. In other words, the muscles contract but the joint involved doesn't move.

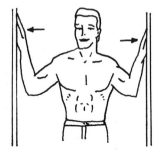

Figure II. 3. *Isometric Contraction.*

Typically, when performing *isometric exercises*, you contract the muscles for 6 to 10 seconds without relaxing. Isometric exercises should be practiced at several different joint angles because the training effect tends to occur primarily at the angle selected for training. Contractions should be repeated one to five times during each training session and training sessions should be scheduled on alternate days.

Advantages of isometric training
    * Since no equipment is required, there is little or no cost.

    * Only a small space is needed for exercise.

    * Isometric training is convenient.

Disadvantages of isometric training
    * Strength isn't developed throughout the full *range of motion*.

    * Progress is difficult to measure unless a dynamometer or tensiometer is available.

    * Training sessions are likely to become boring. There may not be much sense of achievement. It may be harder to stay motivated.

    * Isometric muscle contractions significantly increase blood pressure and are potentially dangerous for people with high blood pressure or heart disease.

    * Isotonic and isokinetic methods generally produce greater strength and hypertrophy gains than isometric training.

ISOTONIC EXERCISES

These are the traditional methods used by everyone from competitive weight lifters to physical therapists to enthusiasts exercising simply to stay in shape. *Isotonic exercises* are those in which muscles shorten or lengthen as they move the joint through the range of motion. Isotonic movements involve both *concentric* and *eccentric contractions*. For example, when performing a dumbbell curl, the arm lifts the weight to the chest. This is the concentric phase (muscle shortens). When the weight is slowly lowered to the starting position, this is the eccentric phase (muscle lengthens). Lowering the weight rapidly limits the potential for strength development during the eccentric phase of exercise.

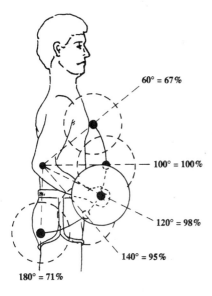

60° = 67%

100° = 100%

120° = 98%

140° = 95%

180° = 71%

Figure II. 4. *Variations in Strength.*
Because muscles acting on the skeletal lever system have weak and strong points throughout the range of motion, the muscle will be worked differently when a movement is performed. In this example, the bicep muscle is weakest at the 100 degree point and therefore is working at 100% of its maximum. At higher and lower points it's easier for the muscle to lift the weight and therefore the bicep doesn't work at its maximum capacity.

Your muscles aren't equally strong through their full range of motion. In any isotonic exercise, there's a "sticking" point. This is the point in the range of motion where the muscle is able to generate the least amount of force. Your movement through the range of motion will be relatively easy until you hit this point. Past this point, movement through the range of motion is easier. The maximal resistance that can be applied in an isotonic exercise is equal to the maximum weight which can be lifted through the sticking point.

Isotonic exercises are usually done by lifting weights or doing *calisthenics*.

Advantages of isotonic exercises

* You develop strength throughout the entire range of motion.

* Progress is easy to follow as more resistance is added.

* It's easier to stay motivated. You don't get bored because there are a wide variety of exercises to perform. And success is more evident.

* You may achieve greater gains in muscle mass (hypertrophy) than with isometric exercises.

* There is less potential for cardiovascular complications.

Disadvantages of isotonic exercises

* Isotonic exercises often require special equipment to provide overload.

* Soreness may result and there is some risk of injury, for example, if a resistance is selected that is too great for the lifter's capacity.

* Most of the strength gained in isotonic training occurs at the weakest point in the range of motion so that the entire range is not maximally trained.

ISOKINETIC EXERCISE

Isokinetic exercises combine the best features of isometric and isotonic exercises. In principle, isokinetic devices can provide maximal resistance throughout a full range of motion. Special machines or devices are required to perform isokinetic exercise. As you apply force, the isokinetic device adapts by adjusting the resistance to equal the force. You can work toward specific strength training goals by doing either fewer repetitions at a slower speed to develop muscle strength or more repetitions at a higher speed to develop muscle endurance.

Advantages of isokinetic exercises

Although much remains to be learned about this relatively new form of strength training (it was introduced in 1968), it seems to have these advantages:

* Resistance is maximum throughout the range of motion, so maximal strength may be obtained.

* Movement can be performed at different speeds, which may be important if you're developing strength for a specific sport or physical activity.

* Isokinetic exercises generally cause fewer injuries and less soreness than isotonic exercises.

Disadvantages of isokinetic exercises

* Specialized equipment is necessary for isokinetic exercises and some of this equipment is expensive. Until recently, it's most often been found in health clubs, spas, universities, hospitals and rehabilitation wards.

* It is possible that an eccentric component may be necessary for optimal gains in strength and hypertrophy to occur, although further research is needed to clarify this issue.

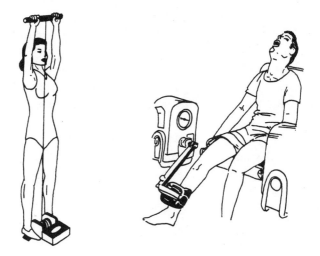

Figure II. 5. *Isokinetic exercise and testing equipment.*

Figure II. 6. *Nordic Fitness Chair.*
Simulates characteristics of isokinetic
equipment.

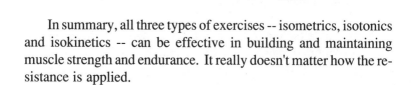

In summary, all three types of exercises -- isometrics, isotonics and isokinetics -- can be effective in building and maintaining muscle strength and endurance. It really doesn't matter how the resistance is applied.

PART III

EVERYONE NEEDS STRENGTH

KIDS AND YOUNG PEOPLE

It is important that children learn the life-long benefits of exercise and fitness. But in addition to an investment in a healthy adult life, kids should know that activity and fitness can also be important in their daily lives. Benefits include looking good, feeling good, greater energy, health, confidence and a positive self-image. A child's fitness level may also impact his or her ability to participate successfully in recreational and competitive sports and other physical activities if that is his or her interest.

Children often have difficulty with activities requiring muscle strength and endurance, particularly upper body strength. In a study conducted at the Institute for Aerobics Research as part of its FITNESSGRAM® program, students performed better on measures of cardiovascular endurance and body composition than on measures of upper body strength and flexibility. The percentage of students achieving acceptable health standards on the fitness assessments was as follows:

	BOYS (N=4,748)	GIRLS (N=4,224)
Health-related Fitness Assessments		
* Body mass index (body composition)	79%	78%
* One-mile walk/run (cardiovascular)	73%	69%
* Sit-ups (abdominal strength)	68%	71%
* Sit and reach (flexibility)	54%	75%
* Pull-ups (upper body strength)	61%	40%
* Flexed-arm hang (upper body strength)	39%	35%

More information about the FITNESSGRAM program and acceptable standards on the health-referenced fitness tests is provided in Part V.

In a position paper in 1983, the American Academy of Pediatrics (AAP) endorsed strength training for sports performance for adolescents. However, in the same paper, the AAP also took the position that prepubescent children (those who haven't developed secondary sex characteristics) could receive only minimal benefits from strength training because they lack the hormones necessary to stimulate muscle growth.

The AAP position paper prompted much controversy. Since 1983, several well-designed and controlled studies have shown improvements in strength in prepubescent youngsters participating in strength training programs. These studies caused the National Strength and Conditioning Association (NSCA) to endorse, with appropriate precautions, strength training for prepubescent youths.

PRECAUTIONS FOR KIDS

The risks of strength training are usually related to training methods and techniques. Studies have shown that persons between the ages of 10 and 19 are particularly prone to injury during strength training. Most of these injuries occur at home. Generally, strength training machines and isokinetic devices are considered safer than free weights for kids, and most children or adolescents can develop adequate strength and endurance with calisthenic exercises, gymnastics and activities such as swimming and wrestling.

In addition to the training principles that apply for adults, these special precautions should be observed for children and adolescents:

* Strength training shouldn't be competitive for children or adolescents. Exercise activities should be fun!

* Strength training programs for kids should emphasize higher repetitions and sets (12-16 repetitions; two to four sets) and less weight.

* A child should be in good physical health and have the emotional maturity to accept and follow instructions before beginning a strength training program that includes resistance machines or equipment.

* Strength training programs for kids should be supervised by competent instructors.

* Children and adolescents should learn to do a variety of calisthenic and strength training exercises. Knowing the purpose of each exercise and how to combine exercises in a logical sequence is important.

* If working with resistance machines or free weights, maximum lifts should not be encouraged.

* Strength training should be a part of a comprehensive fitness program that includes cardiovascular (aerobics) and flexibility exercises.

PROGRAMS FOR KIDS

Insightful and refreshing changes are sweeping across the country in the area of youth fitness testing. These changes are being applauded and embraced by physical education teachers, coaches, and youth program directors in thousands of school districts in all 50 states.

You may have heard announcements in the media that the youth of this country are unfit compared to children of other countries and not as fit as youths from previous decades. Few data are available on comparative fitness levels of youth from various countries. And except for increases in body fatness, children today are as fit as those of thirty years ago. Scientists at the Institute for

Aerobics Research are continuing to investigate this area and are proposing new programs to help children and adolescents improve their fitness levels still further.

You may remember fitness tests from decades ago -- the softball throw, the zig-zag run, the 50-yard dash. While these activities do measure performance, they have little to do with health or general fitness. The Institute advocates instead a fitness test that measures cardiovascular endurance, muscle strength and endurance, flexibility and body composition. To accomplish this, the Institute developed FITNESSGRAM. FITNESSGRAM evaluates performance on these health-related criteria and reports results to students and parents in a new way -- by standards rather than norms or rankings that compare students to each other.

FITNESSGRAM rewards students who try to attain the fitness standards for good health, unlike the fitness tests of previous decades that rewarded athletic performance. As an example, the President's Council on Physical Fitness rewarded students who performed at the 85th percentile or above on all the performance tests. Only about two percent of the students nationwide earned this award. This approach was quite discouraging to the majority of children. It also presented an inaccurate picture of the fitness level of America's children.

FITNESSGRAM rewards exercise behaviors because if the behavior is present, fitness will follow. All children can participate and succeed in this type of program and the behaviors they adopt are likely to last a lifetime. Also, the family can get involved in FIT FOR LIFE, the family program that allows everybody to participate in activities of their choice and earn points for fitness activities.

To get more information about how your school or family can participate in FITNESSGRAM or FIT FOR LIFE, contact the Institute for Aerobics Research in Dallas, Texas.

Rate your child's physical fitness program

At school:

YES   NO

_____ _____ Does he/she participate in daily physical education classes at school?

_____ _____ Does he/she participate in vigorous activities at least 3 to 5 times per week?

_____ _____ Are physical education classes comparable in size to other classes?

_____ _____ Does he/she receive instruction in lifetime fitness activities as well as team activities?

_____ _____ Does he/she enjoy physical education class?

_____ _____ Is he or she assessed annually to measure his or her physical fitness?

_____ _____ Are grades in physical education classes based on knowledge and understanding related to physical activities and physical fitness concepts as well as performance of skills?

At home:

YES   NO

_____ _____ Do you encourage physical activities at home?

_____ _____ Do you set a good example for your child by making exercise a priority in your daily life?

_____ _____ Do you limit the amount of time he/she watches television?

If there is no physical education program for your child at school or if you consider the existing program inadequate or ineffective, take action. Visit with school administrators and teachers. And, emphasize physical activity at home.

WOMEN DURING AND AFTER PREGNANCY

Balanced fitness is just as important for women as for men. As a result, women today are getting involved in strength training programs and enjoying the benefits in health and appearance. In general, precautions for women who strength train are the same as for men. Women who are considering having a child should get in shape before getting pregnant. Being fit can not only help during delivery, it will make returning to form after the baby is born much easier.

In 1985, the American College of Obstetricians and Gynecologists stated that "regardless of prior exercise habits and levels of fitness, most healthy pregnant women without medical or obstetric complications can lift weights safely and beneficially." Specific benefits of strength training during pregnancy include promotion of good posture, prevention of low back pain, strengthening of the pelvic floor and prevention of separation of the abdominal muscles, and enhanced mood and self-image, to name a few.

For the woman who has already developed an acceptable level of physical fitness, it's a good idea to maintain fitness with programs that are modified as the pregnancy progresses. But, only after consultation with a doctor. Based on the recommendations of the American College of Obstetricians and Gynecologists, these general guidelines are suggested:

* Avoid strenuous or exhaustive exercise, particularly during the first trimester.

* Avoid exercising on the back, particularly after the fourth month.

* Avoid exercise in hot or humid conditions or during sickness.

* Drink plenty of water before, during and after exercise.

* Don't exercise when overly tired.

* Avoid taking joints beyond the normal range of motion. Don't twist or apply excessive torque to the body. Perform only slow and controlled movements.

* Don't perform resistance exercises at near maximum effort. Use light resistance and repeat muscle contractions approximately 8 to 12 times. Repeat one to two sets of these repetitions for 10 or more muscle groups.

* Do strength training two to three days per week with a day of rest in between.

* Avoid activities that require balance. Use positions that have a stable base of support.

* Rise slowly from the floor to a standing position to avoid orthostatic hypotension (a sudden drop in blood pressure) that may cause dizziness or a light-headed feeling.

* Breathe in and out on each and every repetition. Be sure to breathe out as force is applied to avoid the *Valsalva maneuver* (breath holding and straining) which might reduce blood flow to the fetus and cause unnecessary and downward forces on the uterus and pelvic floor.

* Empty the bladder prior to exercise and as needed.

PEOPLE OVER 50

For the most part, references to chronological age as they pertain to exercise and fitness are strictly arbitrary. Nearly anyone, regardless of age can benefit from balanced fitness and strength training. There are, however, some general considerations to keep in mind.

As you age, your maximal heart rate decreases. A person 30 years old has a predicted maximum heart rate of 190, while a person 50 years old has a maximum heart rate of 170. (These values can be estimated by subtracting your age from 220 -- providing you are not taking medications that effect your heart rate.) The implication of this decline in maximum heart rate, is a decline in cardiac output (the amount of blood your heart can pump in a given period of time). Reduced cardiac output will result in a reduction of blood and oxygen to the muscles and will impair the ability to exercise.

For most people over fifty, this decline in cardiac output won't have a dramatic effect on their balanced fitness program or functional fitness until they are well advanced in years. It does, however, suggest some precautions. The Valsalva maneuver, for example, is potentially dangerous because it further reduces cardiac output. Good breathing technique while performing strength training exercises is particularly important to this group. Also, it's important for people in this age group to have annual physical examinations.

In general, however, guidelines for strength training for the person over 50 are similar to those of younger people. In addition note the following recommendations:

* Spend extra time warming-up and cooling-down with exercise.

* Low intensities or light resistance should be used when beginning a program, especially for previously sedentary people, and progression should be more gradual than for younger people.

* Because of the increased risk of heart disease and heat injury, older people should be very familiar with warning signals and precautionary measures. If possible, exercise with a partner or in a group.

Warning signs of overexertion

* Pain or pressure in the chest, abdomen, neck, jaw or arms
* Unaccustomed shortness of breath
* Nausea
* Dizziness or fainting
* Irregular pulse, particularly when previously regular
* Extreme fatigue
* Slow recovery from exercise

PEOPLE WITH CHRONIC DISEASES

Chronic diseases are long lasting conditions that require on-going treatment or attention. People with chronic diseases can often derive benefits from strength training and exercise programs just like everybody else. The risk associated with exercise for individuals with specific health concerns will vary widely. It's best to discuss the types of physical activity that are recommended with the health professional who is managing the condition. General guidelines for a few conditions are provided.

PEOPLE WITH HIGH BLOOD PRESSURE

High blood pressure (hypertension) is believed to affect more than 60 million Americans and is a leading cause of coronary heart disease, our nation's number one killer. You have hypertension if your diastolic blood pressure is greater than or equal to 90 mm Hg or if your systolic blood pressure is greater than or equal to 140 mm Hg. These values have to be confirmed by a health professional on several different occasions.

Research studies show that physically active people are less likely to develop hypertension than people who are sedentary. Aerobic exercise has also been shown to lower blood pressure in people with uncomplicated hypertension.

Everybody, not just people with known hypertension, should have his or her blood pressure checked regularly. Anyone who suspects that they might have high blood pressure should see their doctor. Often, there are ways to lower blood pressure without taking medication. If you have high blood pressure, take your medication as directed, follow your doctor's advice about diet and exercise, don't smoke and have your blood pressure checked at least every three months to ensure that it remains under control.

Strength training does not lead to high blood pressure. If you have high blood pressure that is under adequate medical control, you can generally follow the same strength training guidelines as anyone else, with these exceptions:

* Don't do isometric exercises. These types of exercises may cause greater than expected increases in blood pressure.

* Be careful to change positions (standing, sitting, lying, etc.) slowly. You may need more time to adapt to the changes in blood pressure caused by these actions.

* Take plenty of time to warm-up and cool-down.

* If you use equipment, use light resistance and high repetitions for strength and endurance exercises. Approximately 40 to 50% of your one repetition maximum lift is probably about right.

* Avoid the Valsalva maneuver while exercising.

Circuit weight training and exercising with light, hand-held weights (dumbbells) or isokinetic devices are suitable strength training programs for people with controlled hypertension.

CARDIAC PATIENTS

Many cardiac patients need to increase their muscle strength through a program of strength training. Evidence now indicates that an individualized program, if supervised by a physician and conducted within an overall rehabilitation program, can be safe and beneficial. Among the most important benefits of strength training is the increase in self-efficacy and confidence.

Of course, programs must be developed on an individualized basis, but you can probably participate in a strength training program if you meet these criteria:

* You have been a regular participant in a phase III cardiac rehabilitation program for at least three months.

* You have had a recent exercise stress test and your doctor has determined that you have adequate capacity to exercise.

* It has been at least four months since your heart attack or bypass surgery.

* Your blood pressure is under reasonable control (systolic is less than 150 and diastolic is less than 100 mm Hg).

Your aerobic exercise prescription should always take priority. Strength training is supplemental and should be viewed as an extra fitness activity. A circuit training approach to strength training like the one below is recommended for cardiac patients.

* 10 to 12 exercises

* Low- to moderate-resistance consisting of 40 to 50% of one maximum repetition

* 8 to 16 repetitions per exercise

* Adequate rest periods between exercises

Weight machines or isokinetic devices are recommended over free weights for cardiac patients because no spotters are needed and machines are often more time efficient (no changing of weight plates is required).

Cardiac patients should receive a thorough orientation to the equipment, an exercise demonstration and individualized testing before starting a program. And like any other exerciser, the cardiac patient should keep a log to record activities and progress.

During the initial few sessions, blood pressure and heart rate should be monitored at the beginning, during and after the exercise session and recorded in a log. Later, patients can assume responsibility for monitoring their own heart rates. If an excessive elevation is noted, the program may be interrupted. Paying attention to note other common cardiac symptoms (angina, palpitations, lightheadedness) is also important.

Like other strength training programs, progressions are made as resistance levels become "too easy." A major difference is that strength training programs for cardiac patients *must* be medically supervised. If you're a cardiac patient, it is inappropriate, perhaps even dangerous, for you to perform these kinds of activities on your own, at home or in a health club, or without your physician's approval.

If you are recovering from a heart attack, bypass surgery or angioplasty, you should consult a copy of *The Cooper Clinic Cardiac Rehabilitation Program* by Drs. Neil Gordon and Larry Gibbons (Simon and Schuster, 1990) for more detailed guidelines.

PEOPLE WITH OSTEOPOROSIS

A balanced fitness program that includes strength training may help control or prevent osteoporosis, a disease resulting from loss of bone mass. The condition is most commonly found in postmenopausal women and the elderly. Women should begin a strength training program prior to menopause, however, strength training can be advantageous after menopause or after a complete hysterectomy.

Women who are known to have osteoporosis should avoid heavy weights. Light dumbbells or machine workouts are safest. Learning appropriate strength training technique is also important to avoid injury.

PEOPLE WITH ARTHRITIS

Should people with arthritis exercise? The answer is a very definite "yes." People with arthritis tend to have a progressive loss of strength and range of motion. A balanced fitness program is the best way to avoid these adverse effects of joint disease. Remember, exercise doesn't cause arthritis.

Osteoarthritis is most commonly seen in the knees, hips and shoulders. In these joints, as well as in any arthritic joint, it's best to avoid excessive loading or stress. For weight-bearing joints such as the knee or hip, the repetitive pounding of jogging can cause pain, stiffness and joint swelling.

The key to exercise for people with arthritis is to select exercises that challenge the muscles around the arthritic joint without placing undue stress on the joint itself. Jogging is probably inappropriate for people with significant knee or hip arthritis. An exercise that would challenge the leg muscles, take the joint through a full range of motion and is not weight bearing is bicycling. Swimming is often another good choice for people with arthritis. Some people, however, find that the kicking motion in combination with the stiffness caused by cool water temperatures can be painful. For people with shoulder problems, the emphasis should be on range of motion activities. Isokinetic devices are usually safe and effective for people with arthritis in the shoulders.

PEOPLE WITH DIABETES

There are two types of diabetes. Type I diabetes, previously referred to as juvenile diabetes, results because the pancreas doesn't produce sufficient insulin. People with this type of diabetes are insulin dependent. People with type II diabetes are non-insulin dependent and this condition generally begins after age forty which is why it is often called adult-onset diabetes.

Recent evidence suggests that balanced fitness and strength training may help prevent type II diabetes by reducing the amount of insulin required for glucose to be used by the muscles. But what about exercise for the five million Americans who have known diabetes? (It's estimated that an equal number have undiagnosed diabetes.)

Strength training may benefit people with either type of diabetes by helping control the disease, increasing work capacity and reducing the risk of heart disease. The risks of exercise and strength training for people with Type I diabetes are greater, particularly if they have high blood pressure or have developed eye complications as a result of their diabetes.

If you have Type I diabetes, you shouldn't perform strenuous exercise unless your diabetes is under control. Exertion-related hypoglycemia is a major hazard for you. Following these guidelines will help prevent hypoglycemia:

* Don't inject insulin into the limbs that will be exercised, if you intend to exercise immediately after your insulin injection.

* Don't exercise at the time of peak insulin effect.

* You may need to reduce the insulin dosage or increase the amount of carbohydrate intake due to exercise.

* Stop exercising immediately if you note any warning symptoms -- faintness, headache, visual problems, confusion, apathy, nervousness, hallucinations, a feeling of heaviness in the limbs, an unsteady gait, tremor of the hands or hunger.

* Exercise with a partner and always carry a source of carbohydrate.

People with diabetes who are prone to hypoglycemia should know that it can occur as late as 48 hours following an exercise session.

PART IV

HOW TO GET STARTED

THREE STEPS TO SUCCESS

The two most common reasons people give for not getting as much exercise as they need are lack of time and lack of motivation. Of these two, motivation is probably the most critical. But remember "Rome was not built in a day." If you've been sedentary for several years, you can't expect to undo those years of inactivity in just a few training sessions.

The three important steps to help you start and maintain a balanced fitness program are:

* Evaluate
* Educate
* Motivate

Evaluate

Personal evaluation is the first step to achieving your goal of balanced fitness. In other words, you need to know both "where you are" and "where you want to be."

Listed below are several activities that will help you get started. Take plenty of time to complete each exercise. Feel free to write your answers in the space provided.

HEALTH HABITS INVENTORY

This Inventory is provided to increase your awareness of your current health habits and how they may be related to your overall health. Answer the questions, then use your score and the questions themselves to help you examine your lifestyle and changes you may need to make to ensure optimal health.

YES   NO

_____ _____   1. Do you engage in aerobic exercise (jogging, swimming, brisk walking, cycling, cross-country skiing, etc.) a minimum of 20-30 minutes at least three times per week?

_____ _____   2. Do you perform stretching exercises at least three to four times per week?

_____ _____   3. Do you perform strength training exercises (calisthenics or resistance training) or strength building activities (heavy physical labor, gardening, gymnastics) at least two to four times per week?

_____ _____   4. Can you climb a flight of stairs or walk uphill without becoming light-headed or short of breath?

_____ _____   5. Do you eat a variety of foods each day from all the food groups (fruits and vegetables; whole grains and cereals; low-fat dairy products; lean meats; beans, peas and nuts)?

YES   NO

_____ _____ 6. Do you make a conscious effort to limit the amount of fat, saturated fat and cholesterol you eat (including limiting the amount of eggs, shortenings, whole fat dairy products, red meats and organ meats)?

_____ _____ 7. Do you avoid adding salt to your food at the table and limit your intake of highly salted foods?

_____ _____ 8. Do you regularly attempt to eat adequate amounts of starch (complex carbohydrates) and fiber during each day (emphasizing whole grain breads and cereals, fruits, beans, greens and other vegetables)?

_____ _____ 9. Do you avoid eating too much sugar by adding little or none to the foods you eat and by avoiding candy, sugar sweetened soft drinks and rich desserts?

_____ _____ 10. Do you avoid alcohol and caffeine or limit your consumption to one or two drinks per day?

_____ _____ 11. Do you consider your weight to be about right (neither overweight nor underweight)?

_____ _____ 12. When you look in the mirror with a swim suit on, are you satisfied with the amount of fat you see?

_____ _____ 13. Are you a non-smoker and non-user of other tobacco products?

YES   NO

_____ _____   14. Do you find it easy to handle challenges, responsibilities and assignments that are not part of your daily routine?

_____ _____   15. Do you participate in activities that promote relaxation and enjoyment (community activities, hobbies, recreation, church, relaxation techniques)?

_____ _____   16. Are you able to remain patient and calm during stressful situations such as driving in bad traffic or standing in a long line?

_____ _____   17. Can you go through a stressful situation without taking drugs, medication or alcohol?

_____ _____   18. Is the majority of your time free from boredom?

_____ _____   19. Do you usually fasten your seatbelt when you're in an automobile?

_____ _____   20. Do you never drive when you've been drinking alcohol (when you're still feeling the effects)?

_____ _____   21. If you possess guns and weapons, do you keep them secured?

_____ _____   22. Do you keep chemicals, medicines, and harmful materials secured and properly stored in your home?

YES   NO

_____ _____ 23. Do you have smoke alarms and fire extinguishers in your home?

_____ _____ 24. Do you always take medications exactly as prescribed by your doctor?

_____ _____ 25. Do you see your doctor for an annual checkup, even though you're feeling well and aren't sick?

Scoring: Score 1 point for each YES answer.

_____ YOUR SCORE

---

25 POINTS: Congratulations! You're practicing an excellent lifestyle!

20-24 POINTS: You're practicing many positive lifestyle habits and need to make only a few changes.

15-19 POINTS: You're practicing positive lifestyle habits but need to change some of your habits.

10-14 POINTS: You have several poor lifestyle habits that you need to alter to reach a positive level of wellness.

BELOW 10 POINTS: Your health habits are poor and you should seriously consider making positive changes to improve your lifestyle.

ACTIVITY PROFILE

Date_____

This Activity Profile is designed to help you evaluate your level of physical activity. Think about your answers to these questions and look back over your responses from time to time.

1. Over your lifetime, when have you been most physically active? _____
   _____

   What activities did you most enjoy? _____
   _____

2. Are you currently involved with any type of regular exercise program? If yes, what type of exercise activities do you do?
   _____
   _____

   How long have you been doing these exercises? _____

3. Are you more physically active on weekends than week-days? _____

4. Do you consider yourself to be a physically active person in your leisure time? _____

5. Do you have any exercise equipment in your home? List types. _____
   _____
   _____
   _____

6. Do you belong to a health/fitness club or have access to a health/fitness facility? _____

7. Has your doctor ever recommended exercise to you? ____
   _____

8. Has your doctor ever recommended that you lose weight?
   _____

9. What tasks or activities do you perform frequently that require good physical fitness (endurance, strength and flexibility)? List these activities according to purpose and place.

	Endurance	Strength	Flexibility
Home	_____	_____	_____
Work	_____	_____	_____
Play	_____	_____	_____

10. What are your exercise goals? What are the primary reasons you want to accomplish these goals?

GOALS	REASONS
_____	_____
_____	_____
_____	_____
_____	_____
_____	_____
_____	_____
_____	_____
_____	_____

EVALUATE YOUR EMOTIONS,
ATTITUDES AND ENVIRONMENT

What factors in your emotions, attitudes and environment support or block your desire to improve your health and fitness? Once you have identified these factors, you can begin to look for ways to decrease the blocking factors and increase the supportive factors.

SUPPORTING FACTORS   BLOCKING FACTORS

In your *emotions/attitudes*
Example:
* Concern about weight   * Others will see how weak I
                                        am
* Concern about appearance   * _____

* _____   * _____

* _____   * _____

* _____   * _____

SUPPORTING FACTORS	BLOCKING FACTORS

In your *family*
Example:

* Kids will enjoy the activity;   * Spouse says we don't spend
  I'll enjoy time with them   enough time alone together

* _____   * _____

* _____   * _____

* _____   * _____

In your *job*
Example:

* Need more strength to perform   * Must work overtime to keep
  work tasks   up

* _____   * _____

* _____   * _____

* _____   * _____

In your *community*
Example:

* Could make new friends   * Don't know where to go to
                                         work out

* _____   * _____

* _____   * _____

* _____   * _____

After you have evaluated your behaviors and lifestyle habits related to health and fitness, you should assess your current fitness level. Part V includes a variety of tests which can be self-administered that will let you know your current level of fitness and provide standards for setting specific fitness goals. Use the acceptable standards for your age and sex as the basis for setting appropriate fitness goals.

Educate

To help you start and maintain your balanced fitness program, you may need to learn new self-management and problem solving skills. It takes "skill power" rather than "will power" to change behaviors. Problem solving skills are an important part of your balanced fitness program for these reasons:

* Adopting a new habit is seldom a smooth process. You'll experience stalls, plateaus and barriers.

* Because no single routine works for everyone, you need to individualize your program to meet your needs.

* Once you've mastered this systematic approach to improving your health and fitness, you can readily apply the techniques to other aspects of your life -- stress management, personal relationships or even managing your finances.

Part VI of this book provides a wealth of information to help you design a balanced fitness program that will work for you.

Motivate

You've already demonstrated that you're motivated to start a balanced fitness program. You purchased this book! So you're off to a good start.

Your motivation to begin a balanced fitness program probably has to do with your sense of personal responsibility and commitment. You want to improve your health, feel stronger, look better, and be able to function independently for as long as you can. But what will you do to reach your goals?

Don't wait until you feel like training to do it. Decide where and when you will train and what exercises you will do. Study the strategies in Part VI and work them into your plan. Planning for a week at a time works well for most people. You may need reminders such as these:

* Write exercise sessions on your personal calendar. Include aerobics, flexibility and strength training.

* Leave your exercise clothes and shoes near the foot of your bed.

* Carry your exercise bag with you in your car.

* Make a date to exercise with a friend.

* Ask your children or spouse to remind you to exercise.

* Write a contract with yourself to carry out your balanced fitness plan. (See **"Changing Habits,"** page 86)

If writing the exercise session on your calendar and carrying your exercise bag in the car still isn't enough to ensure that you'll exercise, try this: Determine the critical point for you in the decision to exercise. It may be at a certain intersection where you either turn toward the health club or turn toward home. It might be when you first get out of bed and decide to put on exercise shoes and go out for a run or put on house slippers and read the newspaper. For each person there's a different point in the daily routine that's tied to the decision to exercise. Identify yours. It can be a powerful motivator.

Another motivational technique is to record your training sessions. It's important to remember the events, feelings and people associated with your fitness program. Also, keep a weekly record of your weight, pulse and measurements for a year. Copy the **"Exercise Planner"** on page 85 and use it to help you achieve your short-term goals.

As you begin to achieve your goals, give yourself rewards. These questions might help you determine which rewards are likely to work best for you:

* What things would you like to have?

* What things are important to you?

* What would be a nice present to receive?

* What would you hate to lose?

* What do you usually spend extra money on?

* What do you do for fun?

* What are your hobbies/major interests?

* Who do you like to be with?

* What makes you feel really good?

The three steps, EVALUATE, EDUCATE and MOTIVATE, will help you get started on a balanced fitness program. One step is worth repeating -- RE-EVALUATE. There's nothing like success to keep you motivated and help you adhere to your fitness program. Re-evaluate your fitness level every eight to ten weeks and make appropriate adjustments to re-define your goals.

EXERCISE PLANNER

Name _____ For the week of _____

	Time	Activity	Place
MONDAY			

Preparations/reminders:

Comments:

	Time	Activity	Place
TUESDAY			

Preparations/reminders:

Comments:

	Time	Activity	Place
WEDNESDAY			

Preparations/reminders:

Comments:

	Time	Activity	Place
THURSDAY			

Preparations/reminders:

Comments:

	Time	Activity	Place
FRIDAY			

Preparations/reminders:

Comments:

	Time	Activity	Place
SATURDAY			

Preparations/reminders:

Comments:

	Time	Activity	Place
SUNDAY			

Preparations/reminders:

Comments:

	Date	Weight	Waist	Chest/Bust	Hips	Resting Pulse
Beginning						
Ending						

Changing H.A.B.I.T.S.
Personal Plan For Improvement

H. HASSLED, HARRIED, AND UNHAPPY?
What is the general problem area?

_____

A. ANALYZE EMOTIONS, ATTITUDES AND
ENVIRONMENT
What patterns have you identified?

_____

B. BREAKDOWN BARRIERS AND
BRAINSTORM SOLUTIONS
What are potential solutions? Which solutions
are likely to work best? Rate each one
(0 = very low; 7 = very high).

1. _____   ___ ___ ___ ___
2. _____   ___ ___ ___ ___
3. _____   ___ ___ ___ ___
4. _____   ___ ___ ___ ___
5. _____   ___ ___ ___ ___

I. INVOLVE OTHERS AND IDENTIFY A PLAN
Who will assist you with your plan? _____
What are your goals and timelines? _____
I will try solution #__ for __ day/weeks. I will record the following
information: _____

_____
How will you reward yourself?
I will reward myself with _____

T. TRIAL AND ERROR, AND RETRY AGAIN
How successful was your plan?
I attempted the solution __ times. I rate the success of the plan as: ___
(0 = not at all: 7 = very successful)
I will therefore: RETRY REVISE REPLACE the solution. (Circle one)

S. SMALL STEPS BUILD SUCCESS

PART V

HOW FIT ARE YOU?

FITNESS ASSESSMENTS

As a part of your balanced fitness program, it's important to test yourself occasionally to measure your progress. Measurable progress is an important part of motivation. Understanding your current fitness levels can also help you establish goals for making further improvement.

You don't need to go to a physical fitness laboratory or health club to find out your fitness levels. You can do a general evaluation at home or in your neighborhood. In fact, the whole family can participate in these tests. Of course, if you're a member of a health club or the Y, it may help to have a fitness instructor to administer your fitness tests.

If you're male and over 40 or female and over 50, and unaccustomed to regular exercise, or if you answered "yes" to any of the questions on the **"Physical Activity Readiness Questionnaire"** (page 91) or if you're taking any medications, you should get a health screening from your doctor before conducting the self-assessments or beginning any vigorous exercise activity. Even if you do answer "yes" to one of the questions, it's likely that a special exercise program can be designed for you.

TIPS AND PRECAUTIONS FOR PERFORMING THE FITNESS ASSESSMENTS

* If you experience unusual pain or discomfort during any part of the test, STOP IMMEDIATELY and consult your physician.

* Wait one to two hours after your last meal before performing the assessments.

* Wear comfortable, loose-fitting clothing and comfortable, well-padded shoes suitable for walking or jogging.

* Perform warm-up exercises and a well-rounded stretching routine just before beginning the assessments. (See pages 154-157 for examples of stretching exercises)

* If you do the assessments outdoors in a hot climate, test during the morning or late afternoon hours to avoid the heat. Do not perform the assessments outdoors on days that are extremely cold or windy.

* Take as much time as you need to rest between each assessment.

* If possible, have a friend or family member help you with the assessments. It's easy and fun to conduct the tests in a group.

* Practice taking your pulse rate (see page 93) before you conduct the assessments.

* Answer the **"Physical Activity Readiness Questionnaire."**

PHYSICAL ACTIVITY READINESS QUESTIONNAIRE*

YES   NO

_____ _____   Do you become extremely short of breath during mild exercise or exertion?

_____ _____   Do you have frequent dizzy spells?

_____ _____   Do you experience chest pain or pressure while exercising or at any other time?

_____ _____   Do you feel frequent skipped heart beats?

_____ _____   Do you feel frequent racing of the pulse?

_____ _____   Do you ever experience blurred vision while exercising?

_____ _____   Have you had medical problems such as high blood pressure, diabetes, high cholesterol, heart murmur or heart attack?

_____ _____   Do you have muscle-skeletal problems such as arthritis, tendonitis, osteoprosis or chronic back pain that might be aggravated or made worse by exercise?

_____ _____   Are you currently or recently pregnant or are you recovering from surgery or a serious illness?

_____ _____   Do you currently have an acute infectious illness or a fever?

* Adapted from an instrument developed by the British Columbia Department of Health

WARNING SIGNS

Everyone who exercises regularly should be aware of warning signs that may indicate heart attack or other medical problems.

STOP EXERCISING IMMEDIATELY IF ANY OF THESE SYMPTOMS OCCUR AND SEE YOUR PHYSICIAN BEFORE RESUMING EXERCISE:

* Abnormal heart activity -- irregular beats, flutters or palpitation in the chest or throat; sudden bursts of rapid heartbeats; a sudden slowing of a rapid pulse.

* Pain or pressure in the chest, the arm or the throat during or immediately after exercise.

* Dizziness, lightheadedness, sudden lack of coordination, confusion, cold sweating or fainting.

Avoid strenuous exercise immediately after an illness, particularly when a fever is present. Some illnesses, especially viral infections, can lead to myocarditis, a viral infection of the heart muscle.

ADJUST YOUR EXERCISE ROUTINE AND TAKE PRECAUTIONS IF YOU NOTICE ANY OF THESE SYMPTOMS:

* Persistent rapid pulse rate (that is, more than 100 beats per minute) after 5-10 minutes of rest or longer. Reduce the intensity of the activity and progress to a longer period of exercise at lower intensities. Consult your physician if the condition persists.

* Nausea or vomitting after exercise. Reduce the intensity of the endurance or strength training exercise and prolong the cool-down period. Avoid eating for at least two hours before you exercise.

* Extreme breathlessness lasting for more than 10 minutes after you stop exercising. Consult your physician if this condition persists.

* Prolonged fatigue up to 24 hours after exercise. Reduce the intensity of the endurance or strength training exercise and reduce the duration of the workout.

Taking your pulse

In most people, the pulse can be felt wherever a large artery lies near the surface -- at the neck, temple, wrist, and on the chest near the heart. To take the pulse at the neck, temple, or wrist, place the first two fingers gently on the artery. Use the heel of the hand if taking the pulse over the heart.

To take your pulse, count the number of times your heart beats in 15 seconds and multiply by 4. This is your number of beats per minute. If you're taking an exercising pulse rate, begin counting immediately when you finish the exercise since the pulse rate begins to decrease soon after you stop exercising. Move around while taking your pulse to avoid causing blood to "pool" in your legs causing light-headedness or fainting.

15-second pulse rate conversion chart

15 Second Pulse Count	Pulse Rate in Beats per Minute	15 Second Pulse Count	Pulse Rate in Beats per Minute
25	100	36	144
26	104	37	148
27	108	38	152
28	112	39	156
29	116	40	160
30	120	41	164
31	124	42	168
32	128	43	172
33	132	44	176
34	136	45	180
35	140		

CARDIOVASCULAR ENDURANCE

ONE-MILE WALKING TEST

Purpose:

To measure the efficiency with which the heart and lungs can take in and deliver oxygen to the body during exercise.

Equipment:

Watch with a second hand, walking shoes.

Special Considerations:

* Don't drink caffeinated beverages for at least three hours before the test. Caffeine elevates the pulse rate and would affect the validity of the test.

* If you're taking blood pressure or other medication that prevents the heart rate from increasing during exercise or causes it to increase higher than normal, this test would be invalid for you. Don't take this test if you're currently using any of these types of medications:

> Alpha blockers
> Beta blockers
> Calcium channel blockers
> Nitrates
> Combined alpha and beta blockers
> Centrally acting adrenergic inhibitors
> Non-adrenergic peripheral vasodilators

Peripheral acting adrenergic inhibitors
Bronchodilators
Cold medications
Tricyclic antidepressants
Major tranquilizers
Diet medications
Thyroid medications

Procedures:

1. Find a smooth, level surface where you can accurately measure a one-mile distance. A track at a school, a walking course in a park, a shopping mall or even your neighborhood streets. If you plan to walk on the street, avoid stoplights and heavy traffic areas.

2. Warm up for several minutes by stretching or walking briskly.

3. Walk (do not run) one mile as quickly as you can without straining. Maintain a constant pace.

4. After you finish the one-mile walk, keep moving while immediately taking your pulse for 15 seconds. Convert your 15-second heart rate to beats per minute by multiplying by 4. Example, if your 15-second count was 32 beats, your pulse rate was 128 beats per minute. Record your one-minute pulse rate.

5. Record the time it took to walk the one-mile distance in minutes and seconds. Most people take between 10 and 20 minutes to walk one mile.

6. Continue to walk slowly for at least five minutes to allow your heart rate and blood pressure to return to normal levels.

7. See the charts on pages 117-120 to determine your current cardiovascular fitness level.

CARDIOVASCULAR ENDURANCE TESTS FOR CHILDREN AND ADOLESCENTS

Kids can participate in the one-mile test along with adults. Follow the same instructions, except allow children or adolescents to run or walk, whichever they prefer, but cover the mile as fast as they can. Encourage them to maintain a constant pace during most of the test. They often run too fast early in the test and are forced to walk during the latter stages. Record the time in minutes and seconds after the test. Pulse is not taken. Refer to the FITNESSGRAM HEALTH-REFERENCED STANDARDS on pages 125-126 to evaluate results.

OTHER CARDIOVASCULAR ENDURANCE TESTS

There are other tests for evaluating cardiovascular endurance. Several walk/run tests of longer durations have been developed. Tests that have you step up and down on a box to a cadence that increases over time are also popular. However, a trained exercise technician needs to perform this test. Other submaximal tests include bicycle and treadmill tests that increase the workload as your heart rate and blood pressure are monitored. (A submaximal test lets your heart rate increase to only 65 to 75% of the heart's capacity.) These are very safe tests and can be performed at most Ys or health clubs.

The best and most accurate measure of cardiovascular endurance is a maximal exercise stress test on a treadmill. A physician usually performs this test.

MUSCLE STRENGTH AND ENDURANCE

ONE-MINUTE SIT-UP TEST

Purpose:
To measure the strength and endurance of the abdominal muscles.

Equipment:
Exercise mat or well-padded surface (such as a quilt or blanket on the floor), a watch with a second hand.

Procedures:
1. Lie flat on your back on a well-padded surface with your legs together, your feet flat on the floor, and your knees bent. Cross your arms over your chest and tuck your chin to your chest. Have someone hold your feet firmly to the floor or slip your feet under a heavy object. Your buttocks should stay in contact with the mat at all times.

2. Keeping your hands in place, curl your upper body off the floor to the point at which the spine is vertical or your elbows touch your knees. Exhale as you move to the "up" position and inhale as you return to the starting position. This represents one complete sit-up. (See Figure V. 1)

3. Perform as many correct sit-ups as you can in one minute. See the FITCHECK STANDARDS FOR ADULTS on pages 121-122 to evaluate your results.

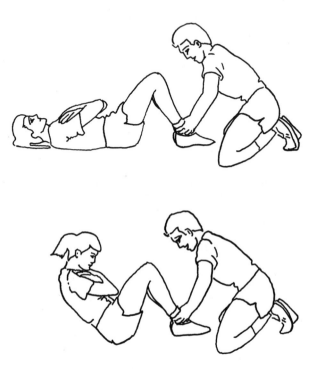

Figure V. 1. *Sit-up Test.*

SIT-UP TEST FOR CHILDREN AND ADOLESCENTS

Kids can perform exactly the same sit-up test as adults. See the FITNESSGRAM HEALTH-REFERENCED STANDARDS to evaluate results.

ONE-MINUTE PUSH-UP TEST

Purpose:

To measure the strength and endurance of the arms, shoulders and chest.

Equipment:

Exercise mat or well-padded surface, watch with a second hand.

Procedures:

1. Place both hands on the mat or floor approximately shoulder width apart. The push-up test begins in the "up" position. From the "up" position, bend your arms and lower your body (keeping your back, buttocks and legs in a straight line) until your chest touches the floor. Then return to the "up" position. This represents one complete push-up. (See Figure V. 2)

2. Women perform modified push-ups with the knees on the floor or mat. They may cross their legs at the ankles or keep the feet apart. (See Figure V. 3)

3. Perform as many correct push-ups as you can in one minute. Refer to the FITCHECK STANDARDS FOR ADULTS on pages 121-122 to evaluate your performance.

Figure V. 2. *Push-up Test.*

Figure V. 3. *Modified Push-up Test.*

BENCH PRESS AND LEG PRESS FOR ADULTS (Optional)

Purpose:

To measure the strength of the muscles of the upper body (bench press) and lower body (leg press).

Equipment:

Bench press and leg press machines that express weight lifted in pounds. (You will need to go to a fitness center, gymnasium or exercise physiology laboratory to perform this test.)

Procedures:

1. For the bench press, lie on the bench with the bar at the nipple line and your hands positioned approximately shoulder width apart. Begin with the weight set at approximately 50% of your body weight.

   For the leg press, sit with your feet on the pedals of the machine and your knees bent at a 60 to 65 degree angle. Women should begin with the weight set at approximately 70% of their body weight and men should begin with a setting equal to approximately 100% of their body weight.

2. Determine the maximum weight that can be lifted one time within five attempts or less.

3. Divide the maximum weight by your body weight.

Example:

Maximum weight lifted in one repetition   =   200 lbs.

Body weight   =   150 lbs.

Strength relative to body
weight ratio   200/150   =   1.33

4. Compare the results to the FITCHECK STANDARDS FOR ADULTS on pages 121-122.

FLEXED-ARM HANG TEST

Purpose:
To assess upper body strength and endurance.

Equipment:
A sturdy horizontal bar (approximately 1.5 inch diameter) positioned at a height above the head, watch with a second hand.

Procedures:
1. Grasp the horizontal bar with an underhand grip (palms facing you). Pull yourself up so that your chin is above the bar and your feet are not touching the ground. If you can't perform a pull-up, have a partner help you or use a bench to assume the hanging position. Your elbows should be flexed and your chest close to the bar. (See Figure V. 4)

2. Time is started when your chin is raised above the bar and stops when your chin either touches the bar, drops below the bar, or your head tilts backward to keep the chin above the bar. Do not hold your breath during the test. The objective is to keep your chin above the bar for as long as possible.

3. Record your time in seconds. Refer to the FITCHECK STANDARDS FOR ADULTS on pages 121-122 to evaluate your performance.

Figure V. 4. *Flexed-Arm Hang Test.*

UPPER BODY STRENGTH AND ENDURANCE IN CHILDREN AND ADOLESCENTS

The FITNESSGRAM test uses either the pull-up or the flexed arm hang to assess upper body strength in children and adolescents. Boys or girls may take either test. Over 50% of all boys and girls will not be able to complete one pull-up. This doesn't mean they have no upper body strength. For those children, simply use the flexed-arm hang to provide a baseline for measuring their strength.

PULL-UP TEST FOR CHILDREN AND ADOLESCENTS
Equipment:

A sturdy horizontal bar (approximately 1.5 inch diameter) at a height that allows the child to hang with his/her arms and legs fully extended and with the feet clear of the floor.

Procedures:

1. Have the child assume a hanging position with an overhand grip (palms facing away from the body). You may need to lift the child to the starting position and spot him/her so he/she doesn't fall at the end of the test.

2. The child uses the arms to pull the body up until the chin is over the bar without touching it and then lowers the body again into the full hanging position. The body shouldn't swing during the movement and pull-ups must be smooth and not done with a kicking or jerky motion. (See Figure V. 5)

3. The exercise is repeated as many times as possible. There is no time limit.

4. Record the number of pull-ups that are performed and compare the results to the FITNESSGRAM HEALTH-REFERENCED STANDARDS on pages 125-126 to evaluate results.

Figure V. 5. *Pull-up Test.*

FLEXED-ARM HANG FOR CHILDREN
AND ADOLESCENTS

Kids can perform the flexed-arm hang test in exactly the same way as adults. You may need to lift the child off the floor to begin the test and spot him/her so that he/she doesn't fall at the end of the test. Record the number of seconds the child is able to maintain the correct hanging position. See the FITNESSGRAM HEALTH-REFERENCED STANDARDS on page 125-126 to evaluate results.

FLEXIBILITY

SIT AND REACH TEST

Purpose:

To measure the flexibility of the lower back and hamstring muscles.

Equipment:

Masking tape and yardstick.

Procedures:

1. Apply a piece of masking tape approximately 12 inches long to the floor. Place a yardstick on the floor perpendicular to the tape so the 15 inch mark is flush with the edge of the tape. Place several pieces of tape over the yardstick to secure it in place.

2. Perform a few stretches to warm-up before you begin this test.

3. With your shoes off, sit on the floor with your legs straight and straddle the yardstick. Keep your feet as close together as possible and your heels flush with the edge of the masking tape. The "0" end of the yardstick should be closest to your groin.

4. With one hand on top of the other and the tips of the middle fingers even, lean forward slowly with the legs straight and reach as far forward along the yardstick as you can. Exhale as you perform the stretch. Be sure to keep your legs straight and don't bend the knees. (See Figure V. 6)

5. Hold the position for at least one second. DO NOT bounce down rapidly. Your score is the point at which the fingertips touch the yardstick at the maximum reach and is recorded in inches to the nearest 1/4 inch. Perform the stretch three times and use the best of the three scores. Compare your results to the FITCHECK STANDARDS FOR ADULTS on page 123-124 to evaluate your performance.

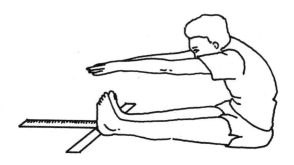

Figure V. 6. *Sit and Reach Test.*

SHOULDER FLEXIBILITY TEST FOR ADULTS

Purpose:

To measure the flexibility of the upper body and shoulders.

Equipment:

Measuring tape.

Procedures:

1. Stand and place your right hand over your right shoulder with the palm of your hand against your back. Reach down as far as possible. At the same time, place your left hand behind your back at the waistline with the back of the hand against the back and reach up as far as possible. (See Figure V. 7A)

2. Have your partner measure the distance between the tips of the right and the left middle fingers and record the value in inches as a negative number if the fingers don't touch. If your fingers overlap, record the value in inches as a positive number. If your fingers touch exactly, record 0.

3. Repeat the test with the left hand coming from above and the right hand coming from below. (See Figure V. 7B)

4. Compare your results to the FITCHECK STANDARDS FOR ADULTS on pages 123-124 to evaluate your performance.

Figure V. 7A. *Right Shoulder Flexibility Test*

Figure V. 7B. *Left Shoulder Flexibility Test*

FLEXIBILITY TEST FOR CHILDREN AND ADOLESCENTS

Kids can perform the sit and reach test just as adults. Move the yardstick so that the 9 inch mark is flush with the edge of the tape. Allow four stretches and record the distance to the nearest 1/2 inch on the fourth trial. See the FITNESSGRAM HEALTH-REFERENCED STANDARDS on pages 125-126 to evaluate the results.

BODY COMPOSITION

Body composition is an important component of health-related fitness. Good body composition results from aerobic activity, strength training and proper diet.

WAIST-TO-HIP RATIO

Purpose:

To evaluate the distribution of fat on the body. The higher the waist-to-hip ratio, the greater the risk of certain diseases such as cardiovascular diseases and non-insulin dependent diabetes.

Equipment:

Cloth tape measure.

Procedures:

Note: It is best to obtain these measurements without clothing or in underwear. You may want to take these measurements in front of a mirror or have a partner take your measurements.

Waist measurement

1. Stand very straight with your abdomen relaxed and your feet together.

2. Place the cloth tape measure around your body in a horizontal plane at the level of your natural waist. This should be the *narrowest* part of your torso (See Figure V. 8). Don't

measure the waist at the level of the umbilicus (navel) -- this value would be too great.

3. The measurement should be taken at the end of a normal breath (exhale) and the tape shouldn't compress the skin.

4. Record the value to the nearest 1/4 inch.

Figure V. 8. *Waist Measurement.*

Hip measurement

1. Stand very straight with your abdomen relaxed and your feet together.

2. Place the cloth tape measure around your hips in a horizontal plane at the level of the maximum (widest) extension of the buttocks. (See Figure V. 9)

3. The tape shouldn't compress the skin.

4. Record the value to the nearest 1/4 inch.

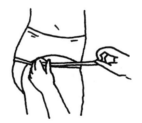

Figure V. 9. *Hip Measurement.*

Divide the waist measurement in inches by the hip measurement in inches to obtain a ratio.

Example:

Waist = 27 inches

Hip   = 37 inches

Ratio = .73

See the FITCHECK STANDARDS FOR ADULTS on pages 123-124 to evaluate your results.

BODY MASS INDEX

Purpose:

To assess overall body fatness. (The body mass index should not be confused with a measure of body composition that is expressed as percent of body fat.)

Equipment:

Weighing scale, yardstick, calculator.

Procedure:

Note:

Both height and weight measurements should be taken without shoes.

Weight

1. Place the scale on a flat, hard, uncarpeted surface.

2. You should wear minimal clothing and no shoes.

3. Record your weight to the nearest 1/2 pound.

Height

1. Stand very straight with the back against a wall, eyes straight ahead and your buttocks, shoulders and the back of your head touching the wall. Your heels should be together.

2. Mark your height at a right angle to the wall. Measure straight back from the crown of your head.

3. Record your height to the nearest 1/4 inch.

Use weight and height to determine body mass index as follows:

1. Convert weight in pounds to weight in kilograms.
   2.2 lbs. = 1 kg.

2. Convert height in inches to centimeters and multiply by 100.
   1 in. = 2.54 cm.

3. Square the height in meters (multiple the number by itself).

4. Divide body weight in kilograms by height in meters squared.

5. See the FITCHECK STANDARDS FOR ADULTS on pages 123-124 to evaluate your results.

Example:

Weight in pounds = 154/2.2 = 70 kg.

Height in inches = 68 X 2.54 X 100 = 1.73 m.

Height in meters squared = 1.73 X 1.73 = 2.99 m^2.

Body Mass Index = 70 kg. / 2.99 m^2 = 23.41

BODY MASS INDEX FOR CHILDREN AND ADOLESCENTS

Obtain measurements and compute the body mass index using the same formula as for adults. See the FITNESSGRAM HEALTH-REFERENCED STANDARDS on pages 125-126 to evaluate body mass index for children and adolescents.

OTHER MEASURES OF BODY COMPOSITION

There are a number of ways to estimate body composition in adults as well as children and adolescents. Underwater weighing is one of the more accurate and valid methods. Skinfold thickness taken at a minimum of three sites on the body is also a recommended way to determine percentage of body fat. A specially trained technician must take these measurements. All of these measures have some margin of error. Determining your body mass index and your waist to hip ratio are excellent ways for you to easily evaluate your body composition.

ADULT FITNESS REPORT CARD

Name _____ Age _____

Date _____

ASSESSMENT	Your Results	Acceptable Level	Goal	Retest Level
Cardiovascular Endurance				
* *One-Mile Walking Test*				
- Time (min./sec.)				
- Pulse (beats/min.)				
Muscular Strength and Endurance				
* *Sit-Ups* (number)				
* *Push-Ups* (number)				
* *Flexed-Arm Hang* (seconds)				
* *Bench Press* (optional)				
- Maximum repetition				
- Body weight				
* *Leg Press* (optional)				
- Maximum repetition				
- Body weight				
Flexibility				
* *Sit and Reach* (inches)				
* *Shoulder Flexibility* (inches)				
Body Composition				
* *Waist-to-Hip Ratio*				
- Waist (inches)				
- Hip (inches)				
* *Body Mass Index*				
- Height (inches)				
- Weight (inches)				

YOUTH FITNESS REPORT CARD

Name _____ Age _____
Date _____

ASSESSMENT	Your Results	Acceptable Level	Goal	Retest Level
Cardiovascular Endurance * *One-Mile Walk/Run* (min./sec.)				
Upper Body Strength and Endurance * *Sit-Ups* (number) * *Pull-Ups* (number) * *Flexed-Arm Hang* (seconds)				
Flexibility * *Sit and Reach Test* (inches)				
Body Composition * *Body Mass Index* - Height (inches) - Weight (inches)				

One-Mile Walking Test
MEN

Directions:

On the left side of this chart, find your age category and pulse rate. If your exact pulse rate isn't shown, round it off. To the right of this value are the one-mile walk times for "Low," "Medium" and "High" fitness levels. You may need to make an adjustment if your weight differs from a specified weight.

Note that for a given heart rate, the older you are, the faster you must walk to qualify for a fitness category. This is because the maximal heart rate decreases with age. Therefore, for any given heart rate, a younger person is working at a relatively lower percentage of maximum aerobic capacity than an older person.

* Assumes Weight of 175 Pounds

Age	Heart Rate	Low Fitness	Medium Fitness	High Fitness
20-29	110	>19:36	17:06 - 19:36	<17:06
	120	>19:10	16:36 - 19:10	<16:36
	130	>18:35	16:06 - 18:35	<16:06
	140	>18:06	15:36 - 18:06	<15:36
	150	>17:36	15:10 - 17:36	<15:10
	160	>17:09	14:42 - 17:09	<14:42
	170	>16:39	14:12 - 16:39	<14:12
30-39	110	>18:21	15:54 - 18:21	<15:54
	120	>17:52	15:24 - 17:52	<15:24
	130	>17:22	14:54 - 17:22	<14:54
	140	>16:54	14:30 - 16:54	<14:30
	150	>16:26	14:00 - 16:26	<14:00
	160	>15:58	13:30 - 15:58	<13:30
	170	>15:28	13:01 - 15:28	<13:01

MEN

* Assumes Weight of 175 Pounds

Age	Heart Rate	Low Fitness	Medium Fitness	High Fitness
40-49	110	>18:05	15:38 - 18:05	<15:38
	120	>17:36	15:09 - 17:36	<15:09
	130	>17:07	14:41 - 17:07	<14:41
	140	>16:38	14:12 - 16:38	<14:12
	150	>16:09	13:42 - 16:09	<13:42
	160	>15:42	13:15 - 15:42	<13:15
	170	>15:12	12:45 - 15:12	<12:45
50-59	110	>17:49	15:22 - 17:49	<15:22
	120	>17:20	14:53 - 17:20	<14:53
	130	>16:51	14:24 - 16:51	<14:24
	140	>16:22	13:51 - 16:22	<13:51
	150	>15:53	13:26 - 15:53	<13:26
	160	>15:26	12:59 - 15:26	<12:59
	170	>14:56	12:30 - 14:56	<12:30
60+	110	>17:55	15:33 - 17:55	<15:33
	120	>17:24	15:04 - 17:24	<15:04
	130	>16:57	14:36 - 16:57	<14:36
	140	>16:28	14:07 - 16:28	<14:07
	150	>15:59	13:39 - 15:59	<13:39
	160	>15:30	13:10 - 15:30	<13:10
	170	>15:04	12:42 - 15:04	<12:42

* For every 10 lbs. over 175 lbs., males must walk 15 seconds faster to qualify for a fitness category.
* For every 10 lbs. under 175 lbs., males can walk 15 seconds slower to qualify for a fitness category.
< means less than
> means greater than

© Institute for Aerobics Research, Dallas, Texas, 1990.

One-Mile Walking Test
WOMEN

Directions:

On the left side of this chart, find your age category and pulse rate. If your exact pulse rate isn't shown, round it off. To the right of this value are the one-mile walk times for "Low," "Medium" and "High" fitness levels. You may need to make an adjustment if your weight differs from a specified weight.

Note that for a given heart rate, the older you are, the faster you must walk to qualify for a fitness category. This is because the maximal heart rate decreases with age. Therefore, for any given heart rate, a younger person is working at a relatively lower percentage of maximum aerobic capacity than an older person.

* Assumes Weight of 125 Pounds

Age	Heart Rate	Low Fitness	Medium Fitness	High Fitness
20-29	110	>20:57	19:08 - 20:57	<19:08
	120	>20:27	18:38 - 20:27	<18:38
	130	>20:00	18:12 - 20:00	<18:12
	140	>19:30	17:42 - 19:30	<17:42
	150	>19:00	17:12 - 19:00	<17:12
	160	>18:30	16:42 - 18:30	<16:42
	170	>18:00	16:12 - 18:00	<16:12
30-39	110	>19:46	17:52 - 19:46	<17:52
	120	>19:18	17:24 - 19:18	<17:24
	130	>18:48	16:54 - 18:48	<16:54
	140	>18:18	16:24 - 18:18	<16:24
	150	>17:48	15:54 - 17:48	<15:54
	160	>17:18	15:24 - 17:18	<15:24
	170	>16:54	14:55 - 16:54	<14:55

WOMEN

* Assumes Weight of 125 Pounds

Age	Heart Rate	Low Fitness	Medium Fitness	High Fitness
40-49	110	>19:15	17:20 - 19:15	<17:20
	120	>18:45	16:50 - 18:45	<16:50
	130	>18:18	16:24 - 18:18	<16:24
	140	>17:48	15:54 - 17:48	<15:54
	150	>17:18	15:24 - 17:18	<15:24
	160	>16:48	14:54 - 16:48	<14:54
	170	>16:18	14:25 - 16:18	<14:25
50-59	110	>18:40	17:04 - 18:40	<17:04
	120	>18:12	16:36 - 18:12	<16:36
	130	>17:42	16:06 - 17:42	<16:06
	140	>17:18	15:36 - 17:18	<15:36
	150	>16:48	15:06 - 16:48	<15:06
	160	>16:18	14:36 - 16:18	<14:36
	170	>15:48	14:06 - 15:48	<14:06
60+	110	>18:00	16:36 - 18:00	<16:36
	120	>17:30	16:06 - 17:30	<16:06
	130	>17:01	15:37 - 17:01	<15:37
	140	>16:31	15:09 - 16:31	<15:09
	150	>16:02	14:39 - 16:02	<14:39
	160	>15:32	14:12 - 15:32	<14:12
	170	>15:04	13:42 - 15:04	<13:42

* For every 10 lbs. over 125 lbs., women must walk 15 seconds faster to qualify for a fitness category.

* For every 10 lbs. under 125 lbs., women can walk 15 seconds slower to qualify for a fitness category.

< means less than

> means greater than

FITCHECK® Standards for Adults

MEN

	Abdominal Strength and Endurance	Upper Body Strength and Endurance			Lower Body Strength and Endurance
	SIT-UPS	PUSH-UPS	FLEXED-ARM HANG	BENCH PRESS	LEG PRESS
	(#/min.)	(#/min.)	(seconds)	(ratio)*	(ratio)*
AGE					
<30	40	35	50	1.10	2.00
30-39	35	30	45	1.00	1.80
40-49	30	25	40	.90	1.70
50-59	25	20	35	.80	1.60
Over 59	20	15	30	.70	1.50

* Optional, ratio is one maximum repetition (lbs.) / body weight (lbs.)

© Institute for Aerobics Research, Dallas, Texas, 1990.

FITCHECK® Standards for Adults

WOMEN

	Abdominal Strength and Endurance	Upper Body Strength and Endurance		Lower Body Strength and Endurance
AGE	SIT-UPS (#/min.)	PUSH-UPS (#/min.)	FLEXED-ARM HANG (seconds)	BENCH PRESS (ratio)*	LEG PRESS (ratio)*
<30	35	30	15	.70	1.50
30-39	30	25	12	.65	1.35
40-49	25	20	9	.60	1.25
50-59	20	15	6	.55	1.15
Over 59	15	10	3	.50	1.10

* Optional, ratio is one maximum repetition (lbs.) / body weight (lbs.)

© Institute for Aerobics Research, Dallas, Texas, 1990.

FITCHECK® Standards for Adults

MEN

	Flexibility			Body Composition	
AGE	LOW BACK Sit and Reach (inches)	SHOULDER Right (inches)	Left	BODY MASS INDEX	WAIST/HIP
<30	18	1.50	1.00	<27.2	<.85
30-39	18	.25	-1.50	<27.2	<.85
40-49	17	-.50	-2.75	<27.2	<.85
50-59	17	-1.00	-3.75	<27.2	<.85
Over 59	17	-3.00	-5.75	<27.2	<.85

< means less than

FITCHECK® Standards for Adults

WOMEN

	Flexibility			Body Composition	
AGE	LOW BACK Sit and Reach (inches)	SHOULDER Right (inches)	Left	BODY MASS INDEX	WAIST/HIP
<30	19	2.25	1.00	<26.9	<.75
30-39	19	2.00	.50	<26.9	<.75
40-49	18	1.25	-.25	<26.9	<.75
50-59	18	.75	-1.75	<26.9	<.75
Over 59	18	.50	-1.75	<26.9	<.75

< means less than

FITNESSGRAM® Health-Referenced Standards
For Children And Adolescents

BOYS

AGE	Cardiovascular Endurance ONE-MILE WALK/RUN (min./sec.)	Body Composition BODY MASS INDEX	Flexibility SIT AND REACH (inches)	Muscle Strength and Endurance SIT-UPS (#/min.)	PULL-UPS (number)	FLEXED-ARM HANG (seconds)
5	16:00	20	10	20	1	5
6	15:00	20	10	20	1	5
7	14:00	20	10	20	1	5
8	13:00	20	10	25	1	10
9	12:00	20	10	25	1	10
10	11:00	21	10	30	1	10
11	11:00	21	10	30	1	10
12	10:00	22	10	35	1	10
13	9:30	23	10	35	2	10
14	8:30	24	10	40	3	15
15	8:30	24	10	40	5	25
16	8:30	25	10	40	5	25
16+	8:30	26	10	40	5	25

**FITNESSGRAM® Health-Referenced Standards
For Children and Adolescents**

GIRLS

AGE	Cardiovascular Endurance ONE-MILE WALK/RUN (min./sec.)	Body Composition BODY MASS INDEX	Flexibility SIT AND REACH (inches)	Muscle Strength and Endurance SIT-UPS (#/min.)	PULL-UPS (number)	FLEXED-ARM HANG (seconds)
5	17:00	20	10	20	1	5
6	16:00	20	10	20	1	5
7	15:00	20	10	20	1	5
8	14:00	20	10	25	1	8
9	13:00	20	10	25	1	8
10	12:00	21	10	30	1	8
11	12:00	21	10	30	1	8
12	12:00	22	10	30	1	8
13	11:30	23	10	30	2	12
14	10:30	24	10	35	3	12
15	10:30	24	10	35	5	12
16	10:30	24	10	35	5	12
16+	10:30	25	10	35	5	12

© Institute for Aerobics Research, Dallas, Texas, 1990.

PART VI

PLANNING A
BALANCED FITNESS
PROGRAM

YOUR STRENGTH TRAINING PROGRAM

Aerobics, flexibility and strength training are the components of balanced fitness. Because most people have neglected the strength component of fitness, the emphasis of this chapter is on strength training.

As you begin a program to improve muscle strength and endurance, you need to define the parameters of your workout.

* Warm-up and Cool-down

* F.I.T. Formula
   Frequency -- How often to workout
   Intensity -- How much weight or resistance to apply
   Time -- How many times you should repeat each exercise

* Repetitions -- How many times to repeat a particular exercise during a set

* Sets -- How many times to repeat a group of repetitions

* Sequence -- The order to perform the exercises

* Form and technique -- The proper way to perform the exercises

* Rest -- How much to rest between repetitions and sets

WARM-UP AND COOL-DOWN

Just as with aerobic exercise, warm-up and cool-down activities are important for strength training.

WARM-UP

Always warm-up prior to any type of strength training exercise. Exercises that increase the heart rate such as light calisthenics are particularly appropriate. These should be followed by mild stretching to increase flexibility.

Before you begin specific strength training exercises, you should move the joints through the same plane and range of motion that you'll do when you add significant resistance. Indeed, some experts suggest that the easiest way to warm-up for strength exercises is to simply do one or two sets at a very light resistance. This prepares the joint and muscles for the overload that is about to come and will minimize muscle soreness following the exercise.

COOL-DOWN

Take time to cool-down at the end of your strength training workout. You'll usually find that stretching at the end of the workout is easier than at the beginning and you may be able to extend the normal range of motion. And because your muscles are warm, you may be less likely to pull or injure them.

Examples of stretches are provided on pages 154-157.

F.I.T. FORMULA

You already know that to build strength you must overload the muscles -- make them work against greater than normal loads. You can use isometric, isotonic or isokinetic exercises to improve your strength or any combination of the three.

Frequency

You should do strength training exercises at least two days per week with at least one day of rest between sessions. If your muscles have been completely fatigued, they need at least 48 hours to recover. That means the same muscle group shouldn't be exercised heavily for two days in a row.

If you're still sore when you start your next workout, even though you've allowed one day of rest, then you're probably training too hard. Cut back on the intensity of the workout until your muscles have had time to adapt. Remember, work for steady progress, start slowly and build strength and endurance gradually. "No pain, maintain" is the best approach.

Some people like to do upper body workouts on three days and lower body exercises on the other three days. You could also alternate strength training workouts with days that you do aerobic exercises. Regardless of what schedule you select, be sure to leave at least one day of rest between strength training workouts involving a given muscle group.

But don't rest too long. Try not to let more than three days go between strength training sessions because muscles begin to atrophy (shrink) when they're not used.

Strength training schedule

* For maintenance -- work out once each week.

* For improvement -- work out twice a week.

* For noticeable improvement -- work out three times a week.

Intensity

Low-intensity exercises can build the muscle endurance needed for daily activities such as carrying groceries or vacuuming the carpet. Low-intensity exercises such as calisthenics improve endurance for function. Medium-intensity exercises help build the muscle endurance needed for good fitness. These types of exercises allow you to do more vigorous activities without tiring quickly. These exercises also help maintain a healthy back and good posture. Low- and medium-intensity muscle endurance exercises are all that most people need.

High-intensity exercises build the muscle strength needed for high-level performance. Strength training is the exercise of choice if this is your objective. Muscle endurance is primarily improved by increasing the number of repetitions you do rather than increasing the amount of weight you add; however, once you're able to do more than about 30 repetitions you start to develop cardiovascular endurance rather than local muscle endurance.

For aerobic exercise, you've probably learned to monitor your heart rate to judge the intensity of your workout. A target heart range of 60 to 90% of your maximum heart rate is recommended.

For strength training, it 's useful to learn a method of determining how hard you're working. The ***Borg Scale of Perceived Exertion*** has been used for nearly forty years by physicians and exercise physiologists to help them communicate with their patients. The scale provides an on-the-spot description of your sense of effort.

BORG SCALE OF PERCEIVED EXERTION

Rating of Perceived Exertion (RPE)	Description
6	
7	Very, very light
8	
9	Very light
10	
11	Fairly light
12	
13	Somewhat hard
14	
15	Hard
16	
17	Very hard
18	
19	Very, very hard
20	

As an example, if you're exercising at a level that you perceive as being fairly strenuous, you might assign an RPE of 13. If you're huffing and puffing, you would probably choose an RPE of 17.

During the first few weeks of your strength training program, don't exceed an RPE of 13. After that period, you may work (after appropriate warm-up and stretching) at a level of 13 to 15. At the end of your last set of strength training exercises, you may be at an RPE of 15 or 16. If you're exercising for health reasons, it's unnecessary to go beyond 17.

Time

The last part of the F.I.T. Formula is "time" -- the number of times you repeat the exercises. Following is a system that brings together the "frequency" and "time" components of the F.I.T. Formula: the *Strength Points System*. This system is based on the most recent guidelines from the American College of Sports Medicine. Use the *Strength Points System* to monitor your weekly strength training activity -- whether you're using free weights, machines or doing calisthenics.

Strength Points System

* You earn one point for each set of 8 to 12 repetitions of an exercise. (Remember that you may not be able to overload the muscles enough if you do just calisthenics, so be prepared to do more repetitions or modify the exercise to make it more difficult.)

* You must perform at least one exercise in each of the ten major muscle groups.

* You must perform at least one set of exercises two times per week.

Muscle Groups	M	T	W	T	F	S	S
* Thighs							
* Quadriceps							
* Hamstrings							
* Calves							
* Biceps							
* Back							
* Triceps							
* Shoulders							
* Abdominals							
* Chest							
Total							

POINTS PER WEEK:

Minimum	20	10 exercises in one set, 8-12 reps, two times per week
Recommended	40	10 exercises in two sets, 8-12 reps, two times per week
Optimal	60+	10 exercises in three sets, 8-12 reps, at least two times per week

© Institute for Aerobics Research, Dallas, Texas, 1990.

SEQUENCE

In general, you should begin with exercises that work the large muscle groups before proceeding to the smaller, individual muscles. For example, you wouldn't want to work the triceps before doing a bench press. If the triceps are fatigued, you wouldn't be able to fully perform the press. Some authorities recommend working the thigh muscles of the lower body first because those are larger muscle groups. Also, alternate exercises requiring a "push" motion with those requiring a "pull" motion.

Following this advice, you would proceed with your exercises in the following sequence:

* Legs

* Chest

* Back

* Shoulders

* Arms

FORM COUNTS

In strength training, proper technique is safer, increases efficiency and allows you to progress faster. With some exercises you may be able to lift more weight using improper form but you will certainly benefit less than if you used proper form with less weight.

Take the time to learn to do exercises properly. You'll benefit by realizing greater gains and reducing your risk of injury. Never sacrifice form or technique to perform another repetition. Some general guidelines for proper strength training include:

* Lift all weights resting on the floor with the legs rather than the lower back. This technique applies to lifting any object -- a heavy box, a child, or a barbell. Obviously, this rule doesn't apply when performing certain lower back exercises meant to lift the weight using your lower back.

* When possible, keep the weight close to your body during the lift for good stability. However, for some lifts, this may not be possible. For example, as you straighten your arms during a bench press, the weight moves further away from your body.

Keep weight close to the body for stability.

* Breathe properly. Don't hold your breath or grunt. Holding the breath and straining during strength training exercises can produce unnecessary changes in your blood pressure. When you attempt to exhale forcibly without letting air out of the lungs (with the glottis closed), the pressure inside your chest increases and blood returning to the heart has to travel through this region of very high pressure. This produces a sudden drop in the flow of blood to the heart and your blood pressure, which can cause dizziness or fainting. When you exhale, a surge of blood rushes into the heart and blood pressure increases to well above normal levels. This entire process is called the "Valsalva" maneuver and can be potentially dangerous. Try to breathe as normally as possible throughout the exercise. Generally, exhale as the force is applied, whether moving weights or performing calisthenics.

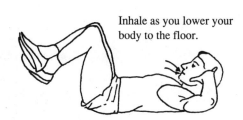

Inhale as you lower your body to the floor.

Exhale as you move to the "up" position of a crunch.

* Work the joint through the full range of motion to build strength and increase flexibility. Maintain control of the weight and be sure to go all the way from fully stretched to fully contracted.

Work through the full range of motion.

* Take your time. Stress the muscle slowly and gradually. Don't throw the weight during the concentric phase or drop it rapidly during the eccentric phase. Allow approximately two to three seconds for each phase.

* Work out with a partner, especially when you're doing high-intensity workouts with free weights. A "spotter" can encourage and motivate, help with lifts, and add weights if needed. Your partner can also help prevent injury if you lose control when reaching the point of muscle fatigue.

SAFETY TIPS

* While exercising should be enjoyable, it's important to concentrate on your workout to get the best results and avoid injury.

* Check equipment regularly to ensure that weights are secure.

* Wear rubber-soled shoes for secure footing.

* Never wear plastic, rubberized or non-porous clothing. These garments promote a significant amount of sweating, which can lead to dehydration and prevent the evaporation of sweat (which can cause heat illness).

* Drink plenty of water before (one to two cups) and during (one cup every 20 minutes or so) your strength training sessions, particularly when exercising in a hot or humid environment.

REST PERIODS

How long to rest between repetitions and sets is an important question that can signficiantly influence the results of your strength training program. The rest period between sets allows time for energy to be restored to the muscle so that it can work again. In circuit training programs, the rest periods between repetitions and sets may be very short. Normally, rest periods vary between 15 seconds and five minutes.

If your goal is to build maximal strength, you'll need longer rest periods between sets. If your goal is to increase cardiovascular endurance, the rest periods between repetitions should be very short. However, if your goal is to improve cardiovascular endurance, you're much more likely to achieve this goal through aerobic exercise than by altering the rest period in strength training.

OPTIONS FOR EXERCISING

CIRCUIT RESISTANCE TRAINING

In circuit training you select a series of exercises to improve overall conditioning (cardiovascular endurance, flexibility, body composition, muscular strength and endurance). Once you know the exercises that you want to do, they are performed in a particular sequence or order. You always begin with the major muscle groups. Never put exercises together that work the same muscles in sequence.

From a cardiovascular standpoint, the most important aspect of circuit training is the amount of rest between each exercise -- the shorter the rest period, the greater the benefit. Typically, rest intervals of no more than 15 to 60 seconds are recommended.

You should keep in mind that the improvement in cardiovascular fitness that results from circuit training is only very modest at best. You should rely on aerobic exercises to develop this component of balanced fitness. According to studies at the Institute for Aerobics Research, the observed increase in heart rate that occurs during circuit training workouts hasn't been found to show improvements in cardiovascular fitness to the same degree as aerobic exercises, such as jogging, cycling, swimming or cross-country skiing.

Below is an example of 10 exercises arranged in a circuit designed to improve strength and endurance in all major muscle groups.

Sequence	Exercises	Muscle Group
1	Squats	Legs and hips
2	Bench press	Chest
3	Crunches	Abdominals
4	Pulldowns	Upper back
5	Leg extensions	Quadriceps
6	Leg curls	Hamstrings
7	Side bends	Obliques
8	Curls	Biceps
9	Tricep extensions	Triceps
10	Dumbbell presses	Shoulders

Training Program

Intensity	13-17 RPE
Duration of each set	25-50 seconds
Repetitions per set	8-20
Times through circuit	1-4
Rest between sets	Minimum
Speed per repetition	Moderate to slow
Workouts per week	2-4

PARCOURSE TRAINING

Originally, parcourses were built on terrain that provided hills to climb, trees to dodge, logs to jump over, as well as stations along the way to perform certain exercises. The objective was speed and endurance. Today, parcourses have been built outdoors, often in parks and recreation areas, to help people combine running or jogging with strength building exercises. If there's a parcourse available to you, you might want to try this type of workout for added variety. Like circuit training, it's an alternate way to combine cardiovascular and strength conditioning into one exercise session.

You may find parcourse training enjoyable as a recreational activity. But, you're unlikely to achieve optimal or balanced fitness from this approach alone because the duration of aerobic activities and intensity of strength training are usually performed below optimal levels.

FREE WEIGHTS OR MACHINES?

Your body doesn't know whether you're using free weights or machines, or, for that matter, performing calisthenics. It's not the equipment that produces the results, rather how it's used. Both free weights and machines can be effective in helping you improve your strength and endurance.

An advantage of free weights over machines is that you don't have to worry about whether the machine fits you. This is especially important for women, children and tall people. Also, there are several distinct advantages to machines over free weights.

* Machines eliminate the need for different size barbells and weights to accommodate different abilities and different exercises.

* Machines save time because you don't have to assemble and re-assemble equipment. Also, in most cases you don't need a spotter as you do when working with heavy free weights.

* Machines let you easily select the amount of resistance you want to work against.

* Machines can provide the maximum resistance a muscle can handle through its full range of motion.

* With machines, you don't have to control the side-to-side movement that free weights require. This advantage may only be important to injured athletes, older people and novices.

RESISTANCE MACHINES AND EQUIPMENT

Resistance machines can be an excellent way for developing muscle strength and endurance. Single-station and multi-station machines are available and costs may range from less than $500 to several thousand dollars.

There are several different types of strength training machines. Machines like Nautilus work on a cam or pulley system. Universal machines use a lever system. These machines apply variable resistance in both the concentric and eccentric phases of the exercise.

Another type of weight machine is hydraulic equipment offered by companies such as Ariel or HydraFitness. These machines work muscles only in the concentric phase. To perform the eccentric phase of the exercise, you must use the antagonist muscle group. This type of machine promotes balance among the agonist and antagonist groups, an important principle of strength training. However, additional research is needed to determine whether the absence of an eccentric phase may actually prevent optimal strength gains from being achieved.

The Nordic Fitness Chair is an example of equipment that simulates the characteristics of isokinetic resistance. These machines allow you to isolate and exercise specific muscle groups. And because of the speed-sensitive resistance mechanism, they automatically adjust to your strength and fitness level eliminating the need for time-consuming adjustments.

Other types of strength training equipment include: rubber bands or elastic tubing, hand-held weights or leg weights of a few ounces to three pounds, barbells and dumbbells. These types of equipment are generally inexpensive. Remember, for any strength training exercise, it's important to select the appropriate exercise and use the equipment correctly to avoid injury and get the results you want.

SELECTING IN-HOME EXERCISE EQUIPMENT

Many pieces of exercise equipment are now available for use in the home. With so many choices, how do you know what to buy? And how can you be sure that "slick" advertising and a smooth sales pitch won't possibly lead you to a bad decision? Keep in mind the principles of overload, progression, and specificity and the F.I.T. Formula (frequency, intensity, time) as you consider exercise equipment.

There are numerous advantages to having exercise equipment in your home:

* Exercising in your home is comfortable and convenient. You don't have to drive to a health club which can save a lot of time.

* Having the equipment in the home provides a reminder to exercise. It's easy to combine exercise with other activities such as watching television or listening to music.

* Once you've invested in the equipment, there are no on-going costs associated with your exercise program.

* The exercise equipment can likely be used by several members of the family. Seeing parents exercise regularly provides a good role model for children.

Some disadvantages of training at home are:

* Maintaining the equipment can be time consuming and perhaps expensive.

* You may not have a training partner to serve as your spotter and help keep you motivated.

Exercise equipment isn't the only answer, though, to getting fit. You still have to do the work. The key is to select exercise equipment to meet your needs, space requirements and budget. With effort and adherence to your routine, in-home equipment can help make exercise a rewarding experience.

SELECTING A HEALTH CLUB OR FITNESS FACILITY

When selecting a place to work out, consider these features:

* The facility should be near your home or work and open at times that are convenient for you. Convenience is one of the most important factors related to adherence to an exercise program.

* The facility shouldn't be overly crowded at the times that you want to work out.

* The facility should be clean, safe, and well-ventilated.

* The equipment should be well maintained and a complete range of equipment should be available.

* The professional staff should be knowledgeable and able to assist you with your individual fitness program. Key staff members should be certified by recognized professional organizations such as the American College of Sports Medicine, the Institute for Aerobics Research, the Aerobics and

Questions to ask when selecting exercise equipment

YES NO

__ __   * Is the manufacturer reputable?

__ __   * Does the equipment come with a warranty? What does the warranty cover and for how long?

__ __   * Is electricity required to operate the equipment?

__ __   * Is the equipment adjustable so that people of different sizes and fitness levels can use it?

__ __   * How much does the equipment cost?

__ __   * Can you perform more than one exercise on the equipment?

__ __   * How much space is required to operate the equipment?

__ __   * Does the equipment come assembled or is it easy to assemble?

__ __   * Is the equipment attractive? Can it fit into your living areas?

__ __   * Is the equipment sturdy and likely to last for several years?

__ __   * Are training instructions/materials provided as needed?

__ __   * Can you achieve the intended results if you follow the instructions and adhere to the program?

__ __   * Do you know anyone who has purchased this equipment?

__ __   * Is there any doubt about the safety of the equipment?

__ __   * Does the manufacturer provide strong customer support?

__ __   * Have you had an opportunity to try it out for yourself?

__ __   * Will this equipment allow you to apply the training principles of overload, progression and specificity, and follow the F.I.T. Formula to achieve your fitness goals?

Fitness Association of America, the International Dance-Exercise Association or the National Strength Conditioning Association.

* The atmosphere should be friendly with an emphasis on fitness rather than "socializing."

Don't forget other fitness facilities that may be available in your community. Schools and universities often have facilities that are open to the public through adult education programs. Check out the YMCAs and parks and recreation programs in your neighborhood. Also, many corporations and churches provide fitness facilities for employees and members.

CHOOSING A PERSONAL TRAINER

Hiring your own personal trainer can offer numerous advantages as you begin a strength training program:

* A specialist designs an individualized program for you.

* You have private instruction with constant supervision to ensure your safety while you're learning to perform new exercises.

* It's motivational and helps you to continue making progress.

Whatever your reasons, there are questions that you should ask to select the trainer who's right for you. Conduct a thorough, face-to-face interview with several trainers before making a decision.

* Is the trainer certified as a physical fitness specialist by a reputable organization such as the American College of Sports Medicine, Aerobics and Fitness Association of American, International Dance-Exercise Association or Institute for Aerobics Research?

* Is the trainer certified in cardiopulmonary resuscitation (CPR)?

* Is the trainer a good role model?

* Where would the workout take place?

* What would the program include? Are medical screenings and fitness assessments conducted at the onset? Is there a gradual progression?

* Does the program follow the F.I.T. Formula?

* What kind of improvement and upgrade is expected after six weeks?

* What is the cost of the program and the payment schedule?

* Is there a contract? Under what condition can the contract be terminated?

* What references can the trainer provide?

FIT FOR LIFE AWARDS PROGRAM

One of the benefits of exercising at home is that the entire family can get involved. Spouses can support each other and children see their parents as good role models for fitness and are more likely to adopt exercise habits that will stay with them for life.

Make fitness a priority for your family by designing your own awards program or use the FIT FOR LIFE program developed by the Institute for Aerobics Research. This program encourages people of all ages to participate in daily physical activity and provides recognition for accomplishments. An activity log and point values for specific activities help monitor progress toward awards.

FIT FOR LIFE Award Rules

1. Each member of the family should have an activity log.

2. Points may be earned from several categories or from one activity.

3. At least two points should be earned in each exercise session.

4. Earn as many points each week as desired. However, only the maximum points per week for each age group will apply toward the award.

5. Try to earn total points for the FIT FOR LIFE Award within eight weeks. If there is an illness or injury, the period can be extended to 10 weeks.

AGE	MAXIMUM POINTS RECORDED PER WEEK	TOTAL POINTS
5-8	10	80
9-12	15	120
13-17	20	160
17+	24	192

FIT FOR LIFE Points Chart

Some activities are more vigorous than others. Certain activities may develop strength and flexibility while others may develop cardiovascular endurance. Select activities for a balanced fitness program. Point values are designed to help record your exercise behavior.

Activity	Time	Points
Basketball	20 minutes	2
Calisthenics	15 minutes	1
Cross-Country Skiing	10 minutes	2
Cycling	15 minutes	1
Dance Aerobics	20 minutes	2
Dance (Tap, Ballet, Modern)	30 minutes	2
Field Hockey	20 minutes	2
Fitness Walking	15 minutes	2
Gymnastics	30 minutes	2
Ice Hockey	20 minutes	2
Jogging/Running	10 minutes	2
Lacrosse	20 minutes	2
Power Volleyball	30 minutes	2
Racquetball/Handball/Squash	20 minutes	2
Rope Jumping (Individual)	10 minutes	2
Skating (Ice/Roller)	15 minutes	1
Soccer	20 minutes	2
Swimming (Continuous)	10 minutes	2
Tennis	15 minutes	1
Weight Training	15 minutes	1
Wrestling (Competitive)	20 minutes	2

ACTIVITY LOG

Record the number of points earned in each activity session in the block corresponding to the day of the week.

FIT FOR LIFE Activity Log

Week	Sun.	Mon.	Tue.	Wed.	Thu.	Fri.	Sat.	Weekly Total
1								
2								
3								
4								
5								
6								
7								
8								
9								
10								

Name _____ Total _____

STRETCHES

There are two phases to a stretch: *active* and *static*. Take the active or moving phase of the stretch to an easy point of tension. Beginning at the point of tension is the static stretch. Gradually apply tension on the muscle, hold it for 10 to 20 seconds and then slowly release.

Perform all stretching exercises slowly and with full control. Never stretch to the point of pain and don't bounce while the muscle is fully stretched. Bouncing can cause injury. Proper breathing is important. Inhale before the stretch and exhale during the active phase of the stretch.

Figure VI. 1. *Chest Pull.*
Stand facing a door frame or have a companion stand behind you. Place hands on the frame at shoulder level and walk through the doorway until slight tension is felt in the chest muscles. Your partner can pull back on your arms to get the same result.

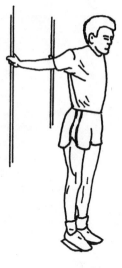

Figure VI. 2. *Upper Back Stretch.*
Stand facing a door frame and place hands on the frame at shoulder level. Lean back and feel the muscles of your upper back as they stretch apart. This exercise is the exact opposite of the chest pull.

Figure VI. 3. *Lower Back Stretch.*
Lie flat on the floor on your back with your legs extended and pull your right knee up to your chest. Press your back to the ground. Hold the position and then repeat with the left knee. Both this stretch and the pelvic tilt are good for improving sway back (lordosis).

Figure VI. 4. *Side Bends.*
Stand with feet shoulder width apart.
Extend one arm overhead and place the hand
of the other arm on the hip. Bend to the side
opposite the lifted arm. Extend the other
arm overhead and repeat to the opposite
side.

Figure VI. 5. *Thigh Stretch.*
Stand facing a wall. Hold the top of
your right foot behind you with your
right hand. Gently pull your heel
toward your buttocks. Repeat for the
other side.

Figure VI. 6. *Alternate Thigh Stretch.*
Lie on your left side with your head resting on your left forearm. Hold the top
of your right foot between the toes and ankle joint with your right heel toward
the right buttock. Repeat for the other side.

Figure VI. 7. *Inner Thigh Stretch.*
Place the soles of your feet together and pull
your heels in as close to the buttocks as
possible. Slowly press the knees down towards
the floor as you lean forward from the hips.

Figure VI. 8. *Calf Stretch.*
Stand facing a wall, approximately
three feet away. Place palms on the
wall and keep feet flat on the floor.
Slowly lean forward as if doing a
pushup.

Figure VI. 9. *Toe Touches.*
From a seated position with legs straight out in front and hands on thighs, bend
over slowly reaching toward your toes. Keep head and back straight as you
move into the stretch.

CALISTHENICS

Calisthenic exercises use the body's weight and the force of gravity as resistance. An advantage of calisthenics is that no equipment is needed. For some muscle groups, such as the abdominals, calisthenics may be the exercise of choice.

The number of repetitions of any calisthenics exercise you perform will vary depending on the exercises that you're doing. As your strength increases, you can modify the exercises to increase the resistance. Using push-ups as an example, here's how to begin:

* Perform one or two sets of 8 to 12 repetitions of push-ups. Generally, if you can complete three sets of 8 to 12 repetitions, but no more, then the exercise is just enough to help you build strength. When you can easily complete three sets of 12 repetitions, then consider making the exercise harder. If you can do more than 12 repetitions in each set, then you aren't "overloaded" enough to achieve best results.

Push-ups are a common calisthenic exercise that develop the arm and chest muscles. Figure VI. 10 shows four types of push-ups that vary in difficulty from easiest to most difficult and can be done anywhere.

1. Push-away (easiest)

Figure VI. 10. *Four types of push-ups.*

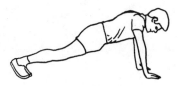

3. Regular push-up

2. Bent knee push-up

4. Advanced push-up with feet elevated (most difficult)

Figure VI. 11. *Forward Lunge.*
Stand with your feet shoulder-width apart. Lean forward, leading with your right knee. Keeping back straight, lower torso as far toward floor as possible.

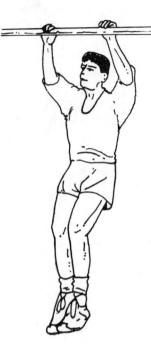

Figure VI. 12. *Pull-Ups.*
Using the overhand grip on a horizontal bar
(palms facing away from your body), begin
from a hanging position with the arms straight.
Pull up until your chin is above the bar. Return
to the hanging position. Exhale when pulling
body up, inhale when lowering body.

Figure VI. 13. *Calf Raises.*
Standing erect, raise up on your toes as high
as possible. Return to starting postion.
Place a one or two inch block of wood (or
book) under your toes for a more challeng-
ing calf raise.

Figure VI. 14. *Chair Dips.*
Extend arms behind body, placing hands (knuckles forward) on edge of a
bench. Extend legs forward so that you are balanced on heels. Lower body as
fas as possible, then raise body by fully extending the arms.

Figure VI. 15. *Sit-Ups.*
From a horizontal position with your knees bent and your arms crossed over
your chest, raise to a sitting position and return.

EXERCISES USING FREE WEIGHTS AND MACHINES

When done properly, resistance training is undoubtedly the most effective kind of strength exercise. Resistance training can be done with free weights or resistance machines. The most important advantage of resistance training over calisthenics is that overload can be adjusted more easily as strength increases.

Use trial and error to determine the amount of resistance that's right for you. Naturally, you'll be able to apply more resistance with the larger muscles of the legs than with the smaller arm, chest and shoulder muscles.

* Find a resistance or weight that you can do no more than 8 to 12 reps and then perform a minimum of two sets of each exercise.

* When you can do 16 repetitions for three sets, add enough resistance to bring you back to 8 repetitions and continue with that resistance until you can perform 15 to 16 repetitions and then repeat the cycle.

Generally, the heaviest resistance you can do for 8 to 12 repetitions represents approximately 75% of your maximum lift (the maximum weight that you can lift one time) which is ideal for developing muscle definition, strength and endurance.

EXERCISES USING MACHINES

Figure VI. 16. *Leg Press.*
Set weight level. Sit in apparatus and place feet on the foot support in front of you. Keep your back flat against the seat pad. With your hands grab the handles on the side of the seat. Extend legs slowly until knees are almost straight, do not "lock" the knee in a straight position. Return weights slowly to starting position.

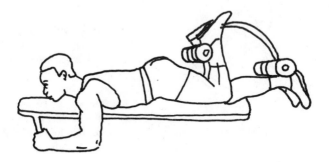

Figure VI. 17. *Leg Curl.*
Set weight level. Lie on your stomach on the apparatus with your knees just beyond the edge of the main pad and your heels under the roller pads. Hold the handles loosely. Pushing against the roller pads, bring your legs up over your back toward your buttocks as far as possible. Slowly allow the roller pads to return to starting position.

Figure VI. 18. *Leg Extension.*
Set weight level. Sit in apparatus with your feet behind the roller pads and your knees just over the front edge of the seat. Fasten seat belt. Hold handles loosely. Using the fronts of your ankles, smoothly push roller pads until your legs are fully extended. Lower roller pads slowly. Be sure to keep your back against the seat pad.

Figure VI. 19. *Calf Raise.*
Set weight level. Attach padded hip belt and adjust it around your hips. Put the toes and balls of your feet on the front edge of the lowest step. Slowly raise up on your toes as high as possible. Slowly lower your heels as far as possible.

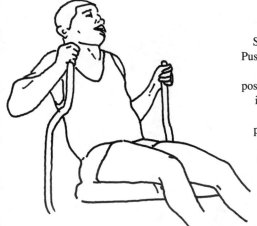

Figure VI. 20. *Bench Press.*
Set weight level. Fasten seat belt.
Push with your feet against the large
foot pedal to raise handles into
position. Grasp both handles, palms
in. Keeping head back, smoothly
push handles forward as far as
possible. With elbows held wide,
allow handles to slowly return
slightly beyond starting position.

Figure VI. 21. *Pull Downs.*
Set weight level. Grip bar with hands
wide apart. With a slight forward lean,
and keeping elbows back, pull bar
down until it touches nape of neck.
Slowly allow bar to return to starting
position. Concentrate on pulling with
lats and back muscles.

Figure VI. 22. *Pulldown.*
Adjust pulley arms of the Nordic
Fitness Chair to the upward
vertical position. Grasp handles
with palms facing forwards.
Pull handles downward to
shoulder level and touch your
elbows to the side of your chest
wall. Pause, and then raise to
original starting position.

Figure VI. 23. *Overhead Press.*
Set weight level. Fasten seat belt.
Grip handles of bar. Push bar
straight up overhead, keeping
elbows wide. Do not arch your
back. Slowly lower bar.

Figure VI. 24. *Arm Curls.*
Set weight level. Sit straddling bench.
Place elbows on pad and grasp handles.
Curl both arms to completely contracted
position. Lower slowly to extended
position.

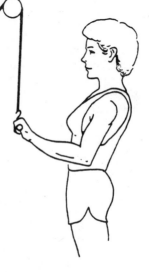

Figure VI. 25. *Tricep Extension.*
Set weight level. Stand facing the
apparatus, grasping the bar with both
hands, palms down. With elbows bent
and held close to body, push bar down to
fully extended position. Allow bar to rise
slowly to starting position.

Figure VI. 26. *Abdominal Crunch.*
Adjust pulley arm of the Nordic
Fitness Chair to the upward vertical
position grasping handles beside the
head. Holding them firmly, draw your
head to your knees, keeping your
lower back rounded. Contract or
tighten your abdominal muscles while
performing the exercise. Return to an
erect position.

EXERCISES USING FREE WEIGHTS

Figure VI. 27. *Squat.*
Rest barbell across your shoulders and behind your neck. Grasp the barbell with your hands, palms up, wider than shoulder-width apart. Keeping your back as straight as possible, bend your knees and lower body into a squatting position. Slowly stand up straight again.

Figure VI. 28. *Lunge.*
Stand holding a dumbbell in each hand, arms at your sides. Step forward with your right foot and lean forward with your back straight, bending at the knee. Step back to starting position

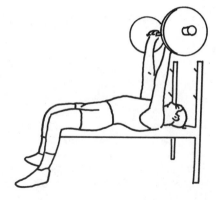

Figure VI. 29. *Bench Press.*
Lie on your back on the bench with your feet flat on the floor. Grasp the
barbell with your hands slightly wider than shoulder-width apart. Begin the
exercise by holding barbell so that it is just touching the chest. Keeping your
elbows close to your body, raise barbell straight above mid-chest level by
extending your arms completely. Lower the barbell slowly to chest.

Figure VI. 30. *Supine Fly.*
Lie on your back on a bench with your
feet flat on the floor on either side. Hold
a dumbbell in each hand (palms up),
arms bent with elbows held out to the
side as far as is comfortable. Keeping
elbows bent, raise dumbbells in an arc so
that they meet over your chest. Lower
dumbbells slowly to level of bench.

Figure VI. 31. *Bent-Over Shoulder Raise.*
Stand with legs shoulder-width apart and torso
bent forward. Hold dumbbells together, arms
hanging fully extended. Keeping elbows slightly
bent and head up, raise dumbbells across front of
body to shoulder height. Lower slowly.

Figure VI. 32. *Pullover.*
Lie on a bench with head just at edge. Grip dumbbell
between thumb and index fingers of both hands, with
arms extended fully above chest. Slowly lower weight
in backward arc over your head, bending your elbows
slightly. Raise weight slowly to fully extended position.

Figure VI. 33. *Overhead Press.*
This exercise can be performed
either standing or seated, in front
of the body or behind the neck
(seated behind-neck is illustrated).
Use a wide grip on the barbell,
palms out. Raise barbell to the
chest level. Extend arms straight
up overhead. Slowly lower bar to
shoulder level.

Figure VI. 34. *Side Shoulder Raise.*
Stand with legs shoulder-width apart.
Hold dumbbells together, arms
hanging fully extended. Keeping
elbows slightly bent and head up,
raise dumbbells across front of body
to shoulder height. Lower slowly.

Figure VI. 35. *Upright Row.*
Bend forward with back parallel to
floor. Grip barbells, palms down,
with hands outside shoulder width.
With legs shoulder-width apart and
knees slightly bent, raise barbell to
chest. Slowly lower to fully
extended position.

Figure VI. 36. *Triceps Extension.*
Put knee and hand on bench. Brace
body with other leg. Hold a
dumbbell in hand, arm bent with
upper arm parallel to floor.
Keeping elbow close to body, raise
the dumbbell so that your arm is
fully extended behind you. Lower
weight slowly.

Figure VI. 37. *Triceps Extension.*
Grasp dumbbell between thumbs
and forefingers of both hands.
Extend arms so that dumbbell is
directly overhead. Lower the
dumbbell slowly in a backward arc
behind the head. Raise the weight
by reversing arc.

Figure VI. 38. *Biceps Curl.*
Sit on a bench with legs apart. Lean
forward and grasp a dumbbell in your
right hand (palm up), bracing your right
elbow against your right leg just inside
the knee. Holding that position, curl the
dumbbell upward completely.

Figure VI. 39. *Arm Curl.*
Using a preacher's bench, sit with arms
extended, upper arms against downward-
angled pad. Grasp a barbell with your hands
(palms up) slightly less than shoulder-width
apart. Curl barbell upward completely. Lower
barbell slowly until arms are fully extended.

PART VII

POINTS TO REMEMBER

POINTS TO REMEMBER

THE STRENGTH CONNECTION

* Moderate levels of aerobic exercise will result in a fitness level associated with a greatly reduced risk of death from all causes including heart disease and even cancer. Just getting out of the least-fit category and into the moderate-fitness category provides substantial benefits.

* Beginning at about age 40, physically fit people have an estimated 20 year advantage in terms of function compared to those who are sedentary. Unfit people will generally reach a level where they are incapable of performing basic living skills long before the fit individual does.

* As you get older, muscle strength and endurance, and flexibility may be as important as cardiovascular endurance to quality of life. Strength to perform daily tasks will allow you to live independently -- bathing, dressing, feeding yourself -- for as long as possible, compressing the period of morbidity before death to a period of only a few days or weeks, rather than years.

* A balanced fitness program includes cardiovascular conditioning, flexibility (stretching) and strength training, and is essential to maintaining functional fitness and quality of life, particularly in the later years.

* It's never too late to start a fitness program, but for optimal results, start early and stay fit through the years. Ideally, you should build strong bones and muscles and a strong cardiovascular system early in life, then work to maintain your physical potential at its maximum.

* The benefits of balanced fitness are numerous and impressive -- improving the cardiovascular and respiratory systems, achieving and maintaining proper weight and body composition, controlling stress, developing strong and healthy bones, and improving appearance and sense of well-being.

* There are many myths about exercise. Look to your physician and other health professionals and voluntary health organizations to recommend programs and resources for you. It's especially important to ask questions if you have special needs.

* The American College of Sports Medicine recommends that healthy adults perform a minimum of 8 to 10 exercises involving the major muscle groups a minimum of two times per week. At least one set of 8 to 12 repetitions to near-fatigue should be completed during each strength training session.

HOW YOUR MUSCLES WORK

* Muscles grow larger and stronger (hypertrophy) in response to overload. Overload is accomplished by increasing resistance, increasing repetitions, decreasing rest time between sets, or increasing the number of workouts per week.

* When an exercise begins to feel easy, in other words you can perform 15 to 16 repetitions without trouble, you should consider increasing the load or resistance. Progress gradually over a period of time to get the best improvement in muscle strength and endurance.

* For best results, attempt to isolate the specific muscles you are working. In other words, make them work without the assistance of other unneeded muscles.

* Achieving balance between major muscle groups can improve posture, ease of movement and reduce risk of injury. The rule of thumb when correcting muscle imbalance is to stretch muscles that are stronger and to strengthen muscles that are weaker.

* All three types of exercises -- isometrics, isotonics and isokinetics -- can be effective in building and maintaining muscle strength and endurance. It really doesn't matter how the resistance is applied. Your body doesn't know whether you're using free weights or machines or performing calisthenics. It's not the equipment that produces the results, rather how it's used.

EVERYONE NEEDS STRENGTH

* Everyone needs strength and can benefit from a balanced fitness program. If you have a chronic disease or special health concern, ask the health professional managing your condition to recommend fitness activities for you.

HOW TO GET STARTED

* Personal evaluation is the first step in achieving the goal of balanced fitness. Evaluate your lifestyle, attitudes, environment and current fitness levels to determine "where you are" and "where you need to be." Compare your fitness level to acceptable standards for your age and sex rather than to rankings of other people.

* Develop a program and plan to meet your needs and keep records of your activities. Re-evaluate your fitness level every eight to ten weeks and make appropriate adjustments. There's nothing like success to keep you motivated and help you adhere to your fitness program. And don't forget to reward yourself for the improvements you make.

PLANNING YOUR BALANCED FITNESS PROGRAM

* Follow these guidelines in your strength training program:
  - Always warm-up and cool-down.
  - Perform one to two sets of 10 exercises from the major muscle groups at least twice a week.
  - Perform sets of 8 to 12 repetitions. If you're working out for health reasons, it's unnecessary to go beyond a RPE of 17. Get a minimum of 20 "strength points" each week.
  - Begin with exercises that work the large muscle groups before proceeding to the smaller, individual muscles.
  - Learn to perform exercises correctly and never sacrifice technique to perform another repetition.
  - Breathe properly and don't hold your breath or strain.
  - Work the full range of motion of the joint to build strength and increase flexibility.
  - Take your time. Stress the muscle slowly, gradually and with control.
  - Allow at least one day of rest between heavy resistance workouts.

* Encourage children and young people you know to get involved in physical activities at school and at home and participate with them. Be a good role model for them by making exercise a priority in your daily life. Design your own awards program or use the FIT FOR LIFE program developed by the Institute for Aerobics Research. This program encourages people of all ages to participate in daily physical activity and provides recognition for accomplishments.

GLOSSARY

ACTIVE STRETCH -- the moving phase of the stretch.

AEROBIC (CARDIOVASCULAR) FITNESS -- the ability of the heart, lungs and blood vessels to carry oxygen to all parts of the body; the result of exercise activities that maintain an elevated heart rate and can be maintained for an extended period of time such as brisk walking, jogging, swimming, cycling and cross-country skiing.

AGONIST -- the muscle or muscles that contract to produce a specific movement.

ANAEROBIC EXERCISE -- short duration, high intensity exercises that rely on metabolic processes that don't require oxygen; examples are sprinting, power lifting and shot putting.

ANTAGONIST -- the muscle or muscles that relax in response to the contraction of the agonist muscle.

ATROPHY -- loss of muscle strength and size; shrinking of the muscles from lack of use.

BALANCED FITNESS -- acceptable levels of cardiovascular fitness, flexibility, and muscle strength and endurance.

BODY COMPOSITION -- describes the makeup of the body in terms of relative proportions of lean body mass and body fat.

BODY FAT -- tissue that stores energy for future use.

BORG SCALE OF PERCEIVED EXERTION -- a subjective scale for judging the intensity of a workout; ratings range from 6 (very, very light) to 20 (very, very hard).

CALISTHENICS -- isotonic exercises that use the body's weight and gravity as resistance.

CONCENTRIC PHASE OF CONTRACTION -- the phase of contraction when the muscle shortens.

ECCENTRIC PHASE OF CONTRACTION -- the phase of contraction when the muscle lengthens.

FAST-TWITCH (WHITE) FIBERS -- muscle fibers that contract at a fast rate, function anaerobically and have great strength but less endurance.

F.I.T. FORMULA -- a formula for planning an effective exercise program in terms of FREQUENCY (how many exercise sessions per week), INTENSITY (how hard the effort) and TIME (how many minutes you exercise or how many times the exercise is repeated).

FLEXIBILITY -- the ability to move a part of the body through its full range of motion; results from stretching exercises.

HYPERTENSION (HIGH BLOOD PRESSURE) -- a diastolic blood pressure that is greater than or equal to 90 mm Hg or a systolic blood pressure that is greater than or equal to 140 mm Hg; a major risk factor for coronary heart disease.

HYPERTROPHY -- the increase in the size of a muscle caused by an increase in the thickness of the individual muscle fibers; a result of strength training exercises.

INVOLUNTARY MUSCLES -- the muscles of the body that are not under your voluntary control; examples include the cardiac (heart) muscle, the smooth muscles of the digestive system, the blood vessels and other organs.

ISOKINETIC EXERCISE -- strength training exercises utilizing devices that adjust the resistance to equal the force applied; examples include Cybex equipment and in-home devices such as the Nordic Fitness Chair.

ISOMETRIC EXERCISE -- strength training exercises performed with muscle contractions against a stationary object or body part; exercises in which the muscles contract but the joint involved doesn't move.

ISOTONIC EXERCISE -- strength training exercises in which muscles shorten or lengthen as they move the joint through the range of motion; examples include calisthenics, exercises with hand-held weights and resistance machines such as Universal or Nautilus.

LEAN BODY MASS -- those parts of the body made up of muscles, bone, nerve tissue, skin and organs of the body.

METABOLISM -- the process by which the body systematically breaks down and converts fat, carbohydrates and protein into a readily usable form of energy; the process of burning calories and expending energy.

MUSCLE ENDURANCE -- the ability of the muscle to make repeated contractions with a less than maximal load; results from high repetition, low intensity strength training exercises.

MUSCLE STRENGTH -- the ability of the muscle to generate force; the result of strength training exercises which apply heavy resistance to the muscle.

OSTEOPOROSIS -- a disease resulting from the gradual loss of bone mass making bones weak and brittle, and increasing the risk of fracture; often occurs in postmenopausal women due to loss of estrogen.

OVERLOAD -- stress that is applied to muscles during strength training; accomplished by increasing resistance, increasing repetitions or decreasing rest time between exercises.

PROGRESSION -- a gradual increase in the load or resistance as muscle strength increases.

RANGE OF MOTION -- the angles and directions through which a joint normally moves.

REPETITIONS (REPS) -- the number of times a particular exercise or lift is repeated during a set.

RESISTANCE -- the load, force or weight applied against the muscle; resistance can be applied with hand-held weights, machines, rubber bands, calisthenics or a partner.

SET -- a group of repetitions performed in sequence; a brief period of rest is allowed between sets for muscles to recover.

SLOW-TWITCH (RED) FIBERS -- muscle fibers that contract at a slow rate, function aerobically and are slow to fatigue; muscle fibers which provide the steady source of energy that is required for aerobic activities.

SPECIFICITY -- the isolation of specific muscles to enhance strength training results.

STATIC STRETCH -- the point of tension in the stretch.

TESTOSTERONE -- the male hormone that stimulates the protein-synthesizing mechanisms responsible for muscle growth; women produce testosterone, but at a rate of one-tenth to one-twentieth of that of males.

VALSALVA MANEUVER -- an attempt to exhale forcibly with the glottis closed, that is, without letting air out of the lungs.

VOLUNTARY MUSCLES -- the muscles of the body under voluntary control; the skeletal muscles that provide the body's support structure and allow for movement.

Institute for Aerobics Research

The Institute for Aerobics Research, founded by Dr. Kenneth H. Cooper, is located on the campus of The Aerobics Center approximately eight miles north of downtown Dallas.

Chartered by the State of Texas on July 6, 1970 as a non-profit, public corporation, the Institute is a research and education center dedicated to advancing the understanding of the relationship between living habits and health. Contributions and grants from individuals, corporations and foundations provide the primary financial support for the Institute's work.

The staff of the Institute acknowledges the continued interest and support of its Board of Trustees and Scientific Advisory Board.